I0755163

Maine Lighthouses

by Harold Stiver

Copyright Statement

Maine Lighthouses
A Guide for Photographers and Explorers

Published by Harold Stiver

Version 1.0
ISBN#978-1-927835-36-4

Index

A Short History of Lighthouses

Lighthouse List

A Short History of Lighthouses

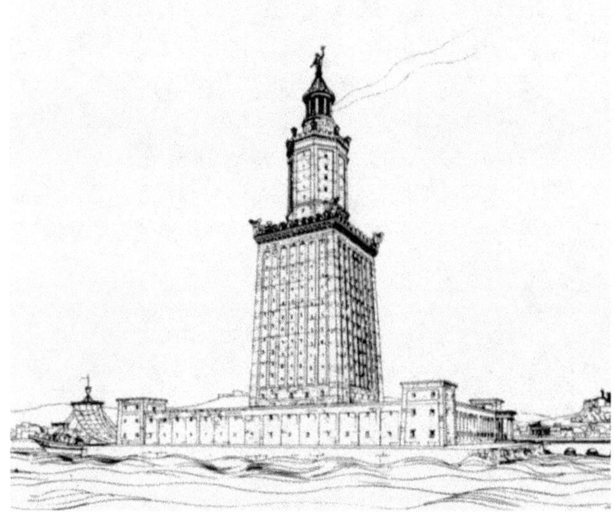

In antiquity, a lighthouse would normally act as a marker to the entrance of harbors rather than as a warning about reefs.

An excavation in Kuntasi, India revealed a square watchtower with a ramp that may have been used as a lighthouse and dating to the 20th century B.C.E.
There is some evidence of a lighthouse from the 5th century B.C.E. of Themistocles of Athens constructing a stone column with a fire on top. This was at the harbor of Piraeus, associated with Athens.

However one of most famous and spectacular early structures was the Lighthouse of Alexandria, or the Pharos of Alexandria. It was one of the Seven Wonders of the Ancient World.

The lighthouse was built in the Third Century B.C. in Alexandria, Egypt by Ptolemy II. It stood on the island of Pharos in the harbor of Alexandria and was said to be 110 metres (350 feet) high.

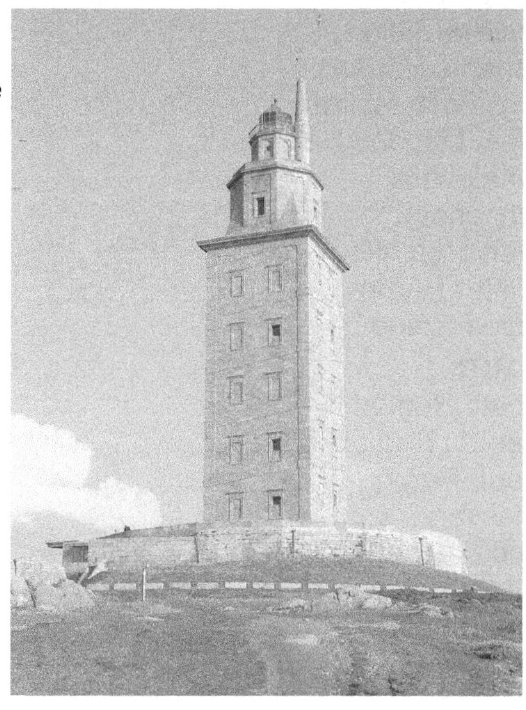

The lighthouse was built in three stages, a large square at the bottom, an octagonal layer in the middle, and a cylindrical tower at the top.
The structure lasted until a series of earthquakes damaged it, with the 1303 Crete earthquake resulting in its destruction.

A lighthouse at Sigeion in the Troad was mentioned by the Greek poet Lesches about 660 B.C.E.

The Tower of Hercules, in northwest Spain, is modelled after the Pharos Lighthouse.

A 2nd century Roman lighthouse at Dover Castle is said to be the oldest surviving building in Britain. It was later converted to a bell tower for the adjacent church

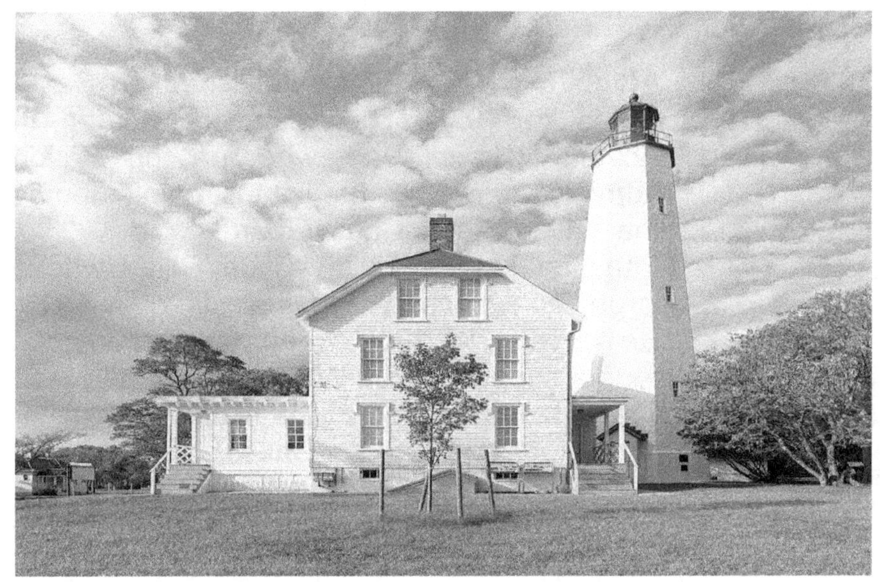

The first lighthouse built in what is presently the United States was on Little Brewster Island in Boston Harbor. It was first lit on September 14, 1716.

Currently the oldest surviving lighthouse is Sandy Hook Lighthouse, June 11, 1764 at the tip of Sandy Hook in New Jersey.

The oldest lighthouse in Maine is the Portland Head Light which sits on a headland at the entrance of Portland Harbor.

Building began in 1787 on orders from George Washington and it was opened in January 10th, 1791.

It was added to the National Register of Historic Places as Portland Head Light on April 24, 1973 and is maintained by the U.S. Coast Guard.

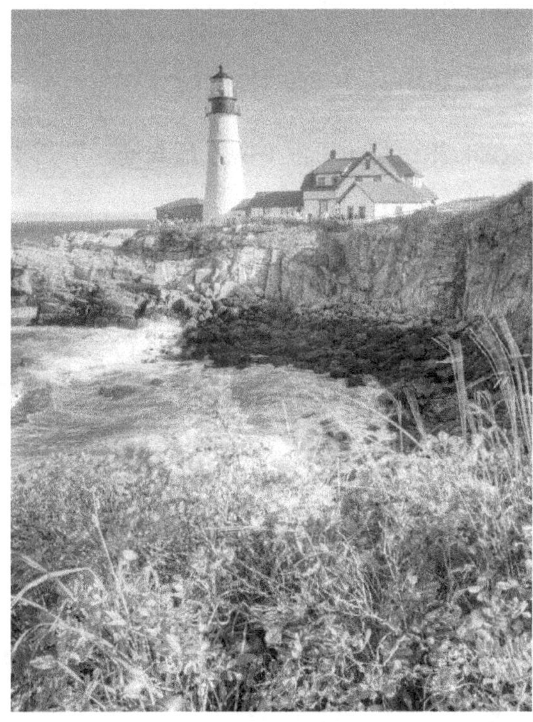

Baker Island Lighthouse

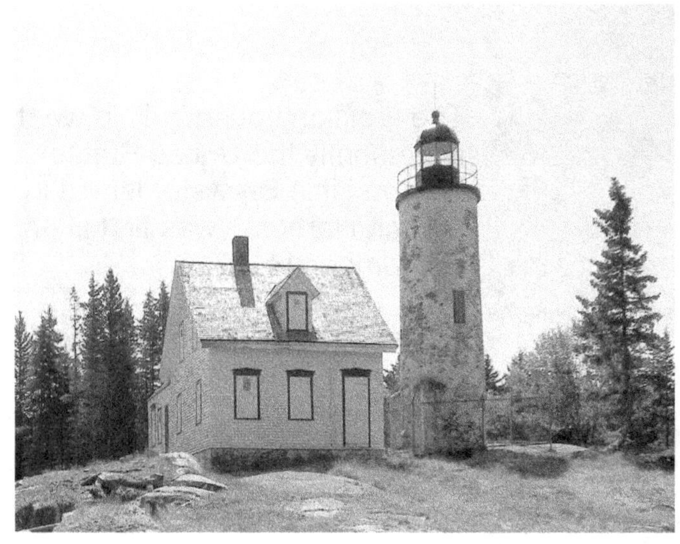

A lighthouse was first established on Baker Island in 1928. The island is located in Acadia National Park who are the station administrators while the light is maintained by the United States Coast Guard.

The first keeper was William Gilley whose large family has settled the island in 1812. He served until 1849, when he was replaced for not supporting the Whig Party.

The light was added to the National Register of Historic Places as Baker's Island Light Station in 1988. In 2017, the Friends of Acadia raised money which has been used to restore the station.

Description: White conical tower

Location: Baker Island in the Cranberry Islands

Directions: Accessible by boat

Coordinates: 44°14'28.6"N 68°11'56.2"W

Opened: 1855

Automated: 1957

Deactivated: Deactivated in 1955, reactivated in 1957

Height: 111 feet

Focal Height: 195

Lens: Fourth-order Fresnel lens

Signal: Alternating white and red 20 seconds

Foghorn Signal: Three second blast every 30 seconds

Visitor Access: Grounds open, tower closed

Bass Harbor Head Lighthouse

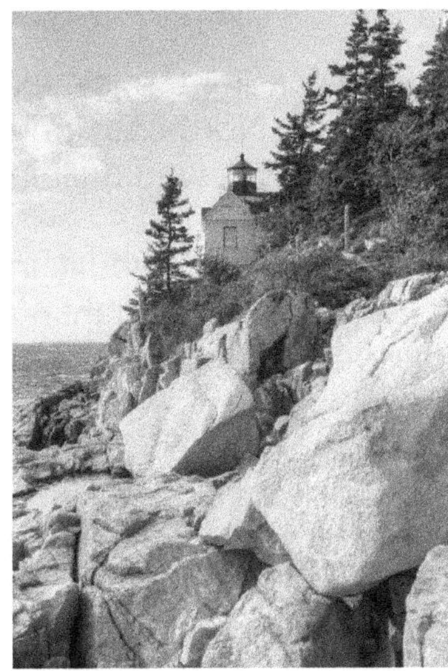

In 1855, the area Lighthouse Inspector recommended that a lighthouse be built to guide ships safely into Bass Harbor. Congress budgeted $5,000 for this purpose and in September of 1858, John Thurston, the first Keeper lit the lamp for the first time.

In 2012 the station was issued on the back of a quarter and in 2015, on a stamp marking the 100th anniversary of the National Park Service.
The structure was added to the National Register of Historic Places on January 21st, 1988

Ownership of the lighthouse property was officially transferred from the Coast Guard to the National Park Service on July 8, 2020

Description: White tower connected to dwelling

Location: South of Bass Harbor in Acadia National Park

Directions: From Bass Harbor, head south on ME-102Alt N/Harbor Dr for 1.2 mi and make a slight right onto Lighthouse Rd where the lighthouse is 0.6 mi

Coordinates: 44°13'18.5"N 68°20'14.3"W

Opened: 1858

Automated: 1974

Deactivated: Active

Lens: Fourth Order Fresnel lens

Height: 32 feet

Focal Height: 56 feet

Signal: Occulting red light four seconds on, one second off

Visitor Access: Grounds open, tower closed

Bear Island Lighthouse

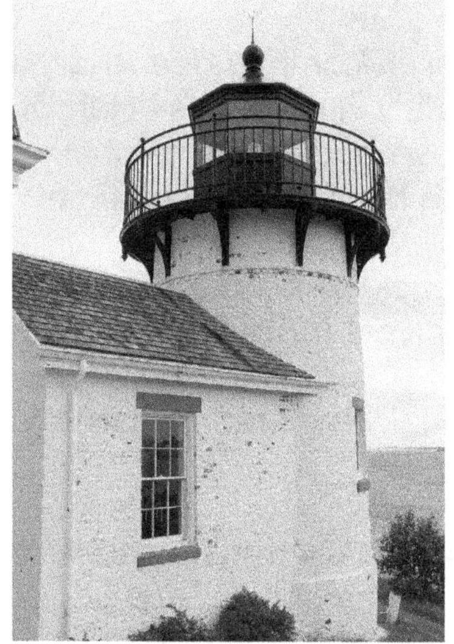

An 1837 survey by the U.S. Navy recommended a lighthouse for Bear Island as needed protection for ships using Northeast and Southwest harbors. This was approved and the station was built in 1839.

The Lighthouse suffered a fire in 1852, but had been rebuilt in 1853. In 1856 a fifth-order Fresnel lens upgraded the lighting system. By 1888, the station had deteriorated to the point that substantial repairs were needed and by 1989 the tower and dwelling had been replaced.

In 1981 the light was replaced by nearby buoys and was deactivated. However it was re-lit in 1989 after encouragement by the Friends of Acadia to serve as a private light.

It was added to the National Register of Historic Places on March 14, 1988..

Description: White cylindrical tower attached to dwelling

Location: Bear Island off Northeast Harbor

Directions: Accessible by boat

Coordinates: 44°17'00.6"N 68°16'11.6"W

Opened: 1889

Automated: 1989

Deactivated: Discontinued in early 1981 and reactivated as a private aid in 1989

Lens: Fifth order Fresnel lens

Height: 31 feet

Focal Height: 100 feet

Signal: White flash every five seconds

Visitor Access: Grounds and tower closed

Blue Hill Bay Lighthouse

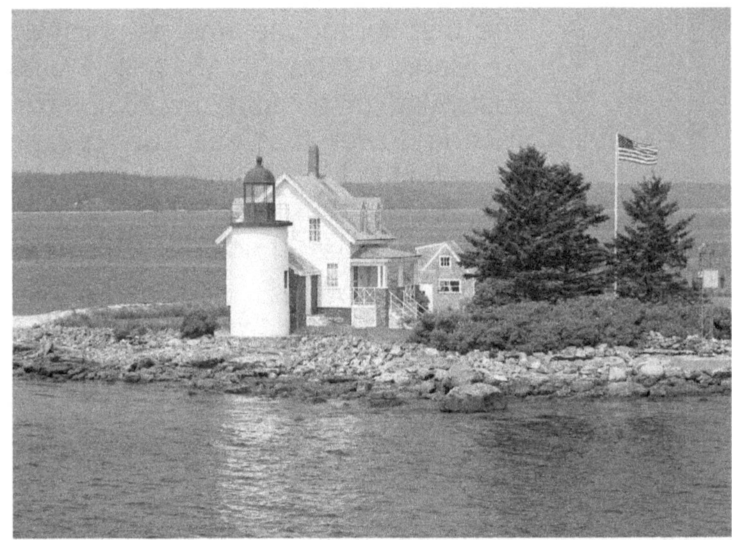

The Blue Hill Bay Lighthouse was built in 1856 to help guide heavy shipping traffic, particularly that associated with the lumber business. In 1890, a two room addition was built on the keepers dwelling. A fog bell was added in 1900. It was operated by a weight which needed to be wound every few hours.

The tower was deactivated in 1934 and replaced by a skeleton tower. The automated light is solar powered.

Description: Skeleton Tower (Original cylindrical tower still stands)

Location: Green Island

Directions: Accessible by boat

Coordinates: 44°14'55.6"N 68°29'52.2"W

Opened: 1934 (Original 1856)

Automated: 1934

Deactivated: Active

Height: 21 feet

Lens: Fifth-order Fresnel lens

Signal: Green flash every 4 seconds

Foghorn Signal: Single, then double every 22 seconds

Visitor Access: Grounds and tower closed

Boon Island Lighthouse

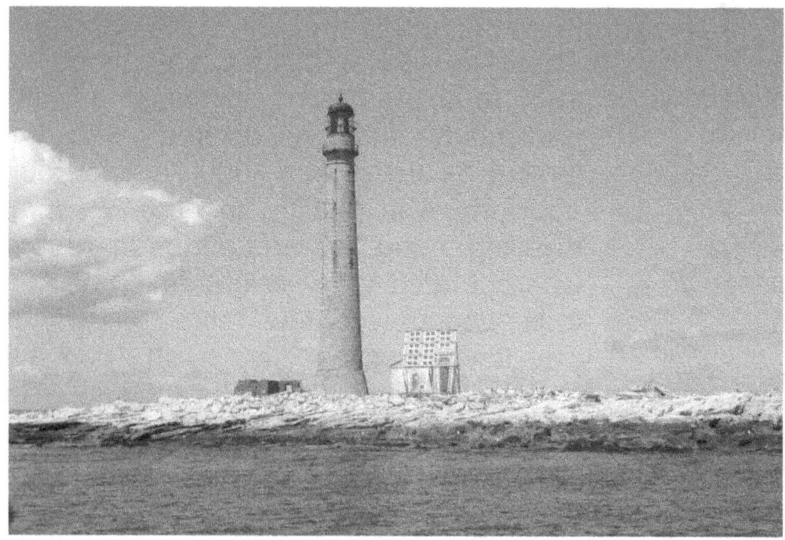

The first lighthouse was established on Boon Island in 1811 but was destroyed in a storm in 1832. The second tower that still survives, is the tallest in Maine at 133 feet.

The worst storm the station suffered hit on January 31, 1898. 100 miles an hour winds smashed the structures, with two water tanks lifted and wrecked, and two outbuildings destroyed.

The lighthouse was listed on the National Register of Historic Places as Boon Island Light Station on March 14, 1988

Description: Gray conical tower

Location: Boon Island

Directions: Accessible by boat

Coordinates: 43°07'17.0"N 70°28'35.0"W

Opened: 1854 (First tower 1811) (Second tower 1831)

Automated: 1978

Deactivated: Active

Height: 133 feet

Focal Height: 137

Lens: Second-order Fresnel len

Signal: White flash every 5 seconds

Foghorn Signal: 2 second blast every 10 seconds

Visitor Access: Grounds and tower closed

Browns Head Lighthouse

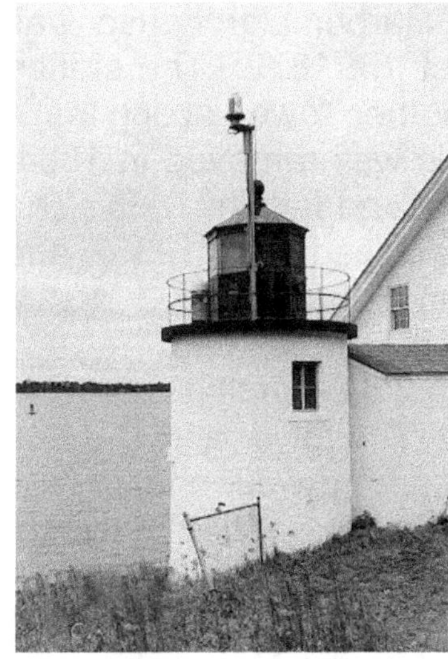

Funds were budgeted for a lighthouse on Browns Head on Vinalhaven Island in 1831 and the station opened in 1832. When an inspection was done in 1842, the station was reported to have defects, including poor quality on the tower exterior. The woodwork on the interior was described as rotting and the tower had shifted due to weather. A new tower and dwelling was needed but it would not be built until 1857.

The station has been listed on the National Register of Historic Places as "Browns Head Light Station" on January 27, 1983.

Description: White cylindrical tower

Location: At the northwestern tip of Vinalhaven Island

Directions: Take the the ferry from Rockland to Vinalhaven Island

Coordinates: 44°06'42.4"N 68°54'34.2"W

Opened: 1857

Automated: 1987

Deactivated: Active

Height: 24 feet

Focal Height: 39 feet

Lens: Fourth-order Fresnel Lens

Signal: White flash between two red ones

Foghorn Signal: 1 blast every 10 seconds

Visitor Access: Grounds open, tower closed

Burnt Coat Harbor (Hockamock Head) Lighthouse

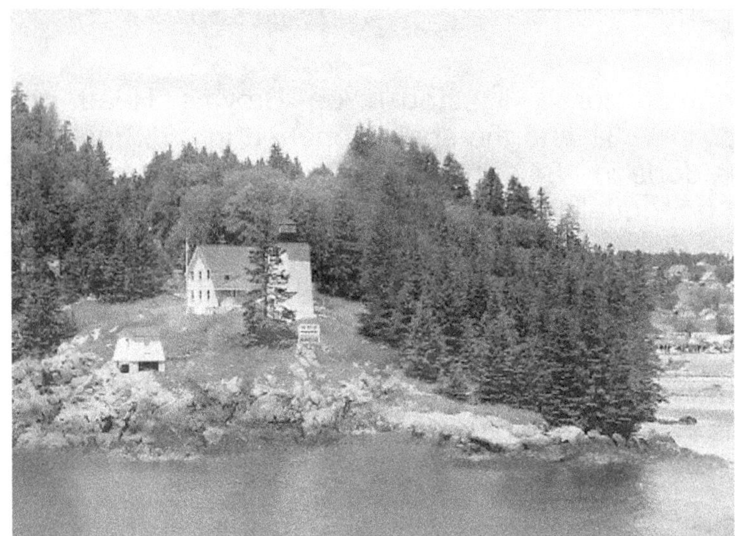

The Burnt Coat Harbor Lighthouse was opened on August 15, 1872. .The station originally had another tower acting as a range light but this was removed in 1884. A boat house was added in 1885. The station was electrified in 1935 and received a foghorn at that time.
After automation, the station had deteriorated but in 2006 funding was found to restore it. The tower and keeper's dwelling are now open for visitors from Tuesday to Sunday between 11 a.m. and 3 p.m. There is also an apartment in the house available for rental. It was listed on the National Register of Historic Places in 1988

Description: Square brick structure

Location: Southern side of Swan's Island

Directions: Take Swan's Island Ferry from Bass Harbor. On Swan's Island, drive 1/2 mile and turn right at the stop sign. Continue for 3.8 miles to the lighthouse

Coordinates: 44°08'03.3"N 68°26'50.1"W

Opened: 1872

Automated: 1975

Deactivated: Active

Height: 32 feet

Focal Height: 75 feet

Lens: VLB-44

Signal: White flash every 4 seconds

Foghorn Signal: One blast every 10 seconds

Visitor Access: Grounds and tower open

Burnt Island Lighthouse

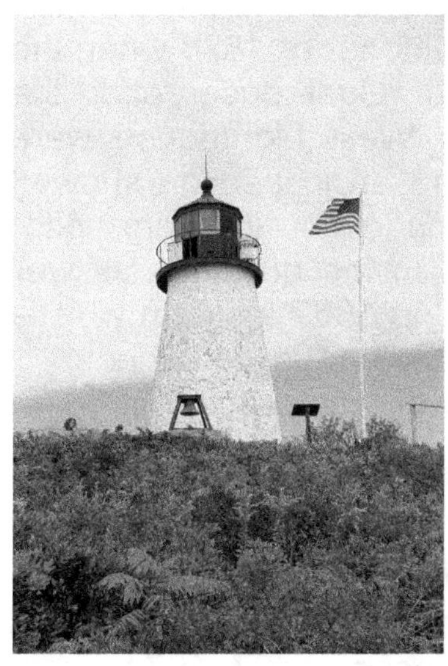

In 1821, local officials and businesses requested the government to build a lighthouse on Burnt Island. It was needed to guide ships safely into Boothbay Harbor. Within a few months, Burnt island Lighthouse was completed and opened.

In 1857 the reflector lamps were upgraded to a fourth-order Fresnel lens

The Keepers of Burnt Island Light is a volunteer organization which has promoted the preservation of the station, including a restoration in 2020.

The light was automated in 1988.

It was added to the National Register of Historic Places as Burnt Island Light Station on November 23, 1977.

Description: White conical tower

Location: Burnt Island

Directions: Maine Lighthouse Museum offers tours

Coordinates: 43°49'30.7"N 69°38'24.7"W

Opened: 1821

Automated: 1988

Deactivated: Active

Lens: Fourth-order Fresnel lens

Height: 30 feet

Focal Height: 61 feet

Signal: Flashing red 6 seconds with two white sectors

Foghorn Signal: 1 blast every 10 seconds

Visitor Access: Grounds and tower open

Cape Elizabeth Lighthouse

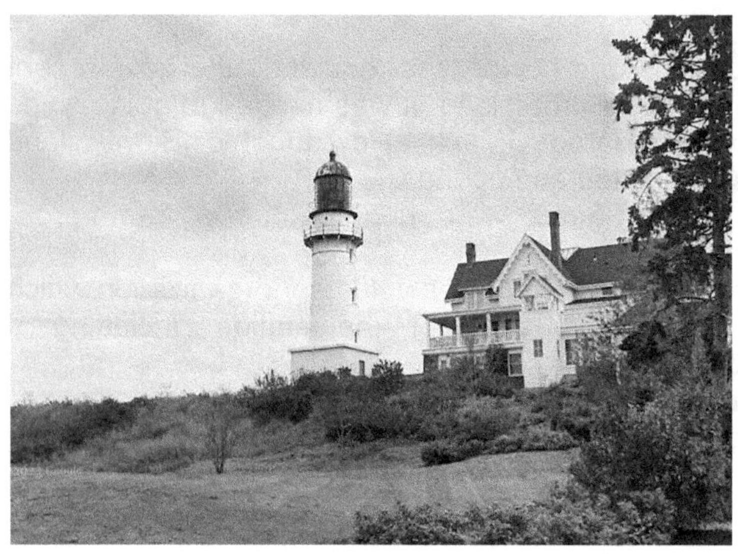

The Cape Elizabeth Station was established in October of 1828 when the Cape Elizabeth Lighthouse and the Cape Elizabeth West Lighthouse were opened. By 1843 an inspection showed that the station was in very poor condition, leaks in the buildings as well as rotting wood. In 1869 a steam whistle was set up for use in foggy weather.

The present tower was erected in 1874, as was the Cape Elizabeth West Tower. In 1924 the West Tower became inactive.

Cape Elizabeth Light was added to the National Register of Historic Places as Two Lights on December 27, 1974.

Description: White conical tower

Location: Cape Elizabeth

Directions: From Highway 77 in Cape Elizabeth, take Two Lights Road SW for 1.4 miles to Two Lights Terrace where the lighthouse is a short distance.

Coordinates: 43°33'57.9"N 70°12'00.3"W

Opened: 1874

Automated: 1963

Deactivated: Active

Height: 67 feet

Focal Height: 129 feet

Lens: Second-order Fresnel lens

Signal: 4 white flashes every 15 seconds

Foghorn Signal: 2 blasts every 60 seconds

Visitor Access: Grounds and tower closed

Cape Elizabeth West Lighthouse

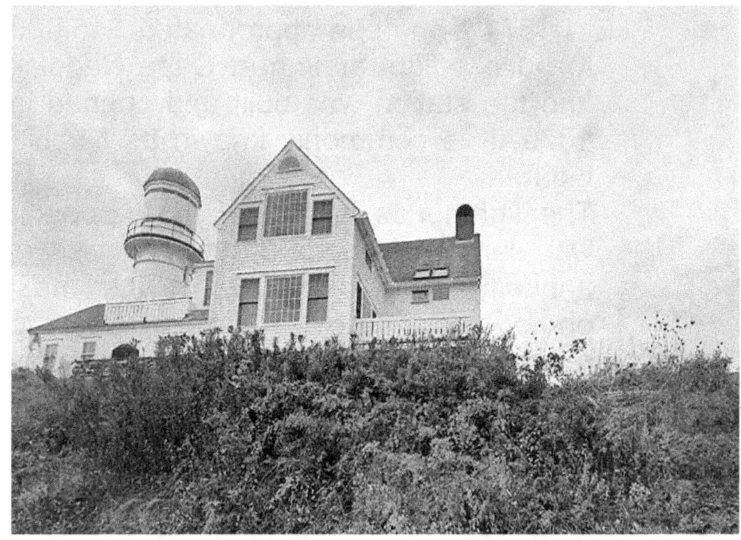

The Cape Elizabeth Station was established in October of 1828 when the Cape Elizabeth Lighthouse and the Cape Elizabeth West Lighthouse were opened. By 1843 an inspection showed that the station was in very poor condition, leaks in the buildings as well as rotting wood. In 1869 a steam whistle was set up for use in foggy weather.

The present tower was erected in 1874, as was the Cape Elizabeth West Tower. In 1924 the West Tower became inactive.

Cape Elizabeth Light was added to the National Register of Historic Places as Two Lights on December 27, 1974.

Description: White conical tower attached to dwelling

Location: Cape Elizabeth

Directions: From Highway 77 in Cape Elizabeth, take Two Lights Road SW for 1.4 miles to Two Lights Terrace where the lighthouse is a short distance.

Coordinates: 43°33'51.2"N 70°12'09.3"W

Opened: 1874

Automated: 1863

Deactivated: 1924

Height: 66 feet

Lens: Third-order Fresnel lens

Visitor Access: Grounds and tower closed

Cape Neddick (Nubble) Lighthouse

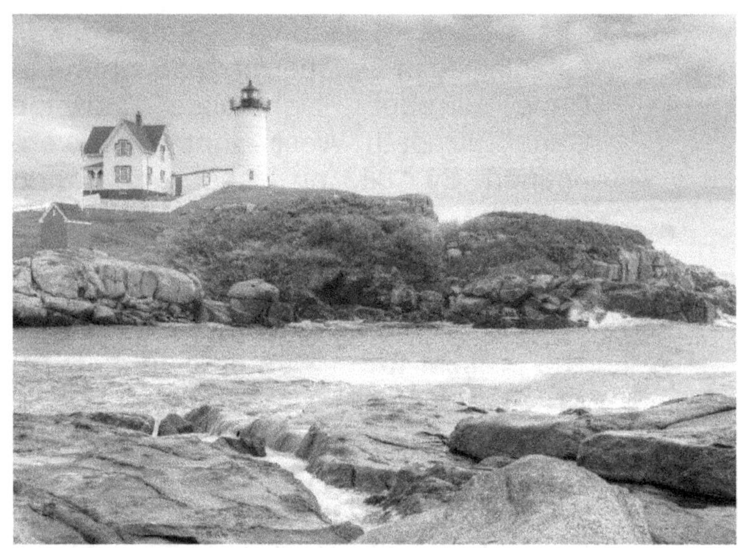

In 1874 Congress appropriated $15,000 to build a light station at Cape Neddick and the station was built and opened in 1879. It is commonly known as Nubble Light.

The lighthouse is one of most popular with large numbers of tourists visiting annually. It is also one of the most photogenic. The station's keepers regularly supplemented their income by ferrying visitors to the island for a tour. The Golden Record on the Voyager spacecraft included an image of this iconic lighthouse.

An extensive restoration took place between 2017 and 2012. The station was registered to the National Register of Historic Places on April 16, 1985.

Description: White conical tower attached to dwelling

Location: Cape Neddick

Directions: Small island off Cape Neddick

Coordinates: 43°09'54.6"N 70°35'28.0"W

Opened: 1879

Automated: 1987

Deactivated: Active

Height: 41 feet

Focal Height: 88 feet

Lens: Fourth-order Fresnel lens

Signal: Red flash every 6 seconds

Foghorn Signal: 1 blast every 10 seconds

Visitor Access: Grounds open, tower closed

Cuckolds Lighthouse

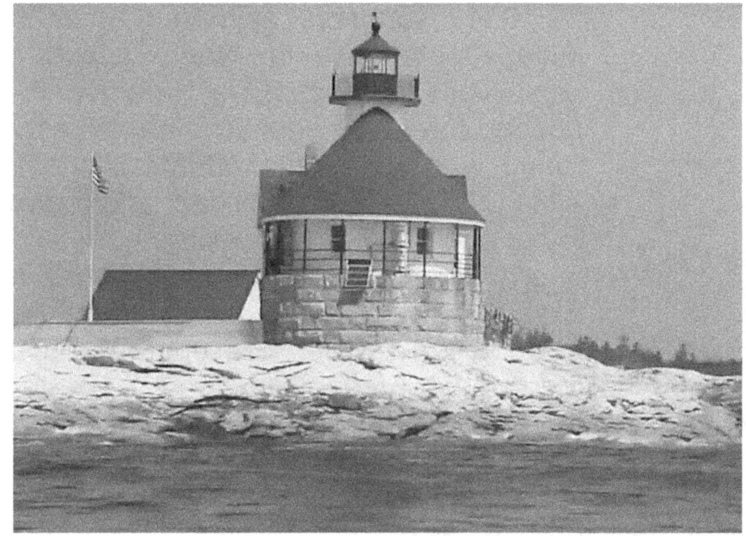

The Cuckolds are rocky islets that rise about 15 feet above the water and pose a significant danger to vessels transiting Boothbay Harbor. Work on the Cuckholds Lighthouse was complete and the station lit on November 16, 1892. A steam-powered Daboll foghorn was in operation a month after. This was upgraded to an oil operated engine in 1902.

The Cuckolds Station was automated in 1974, and later the Coast Guard demolished the boathouse and keepers' dwelling.

The boathouse and Keeper's dwelling was restored between 2010 and 2012. The Cuckolds Light was added to the National Register of Historic Places as Cuckolds Light Station on December 2, 2002.

Description: White octagonal tower on dwelling

Location: Southern end of Southport Island

Directions: Accessible by boat

Coordinates: 43°46'46.2"N 69°39'00.0"W

Opened: 1907

Automated: 1974

Deactivated: Active

Height: 48 feet

Focal Height: 59 feet

Lens: Fourth-order Fresnel lens

Signal: White flash for 1 second, 2 second eclipse, white flash for 3 seconds

Foghorn Signal: 1 blast every 15 seconds

Visitor Access: Grounds open, tower closed

Curtis Island Lighthouse

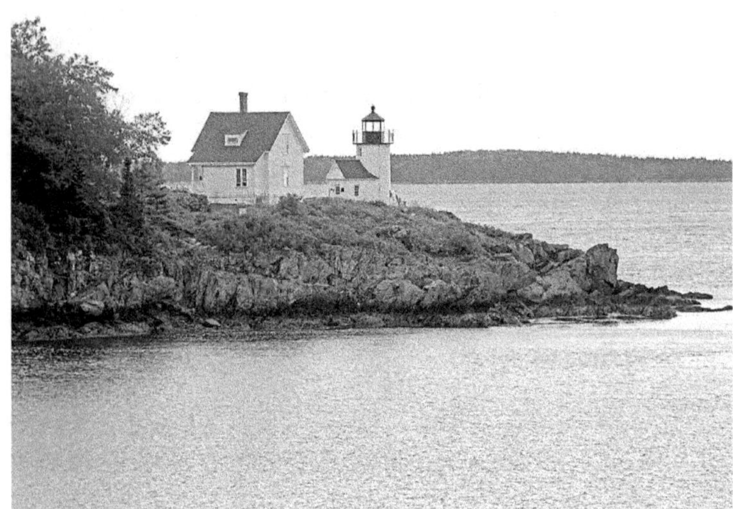

In 1834, Congress approved funds to build a lighthouse on Negro Island to serve vessels in Camden Harbor and it opened the same year. The name of the island was changed to Curtis Island in 1934. The station included a 20 foot tower and a keeper's dwelling.

In an 1842 report the tower was noted to have suffered cracks due to a storm.

In 1856 the lighting was upgraded to a fourth-order Fresnel lens.

In 1896 the present tower was built to replace the original. The light was automated in 1972.

The station was listed in the National Register of Historic Places on May 17, 1973.

Description: Cylindrical brick tower

Location: Curtis Island

Directions: Accessible by boat

Coordinates: 44°12'05.0"N 69°02'55.9"W

Opened: 1896

Automated: 1972

Deactivated: Active

Height: 25 feet

Focal Height: 52 feet

Lens: Fourth-order Fresnel lens

Signal: Green flash every 4 seconds

Visitor Access: Grounds open, tower closed

Deer Island Thorofare (Mark Island) Lighthouse

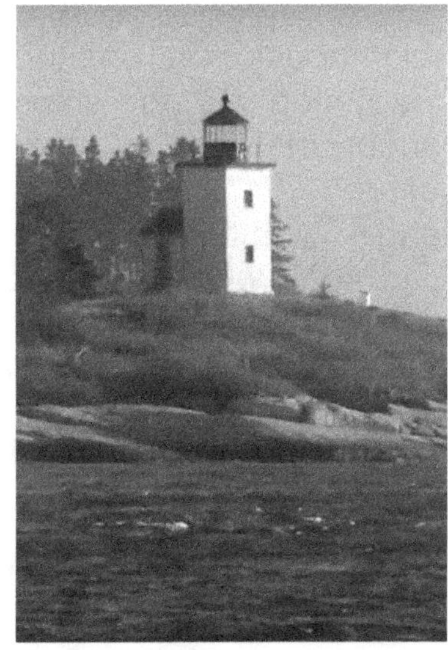

In 1855, it was recommended by the Lighthouse Inspector that a lighthouse be built on Mark Island to aid ships traversing the popular Deer Island Thorofare. Congress approved funding and the lighthouse opened in 1858. A boathouse was added to the station in 1877 and a fuel house in 1895.

In 1958 the dwelling was destroyed in a fire, and it was decided to automate the station rather than rebuild it. At this time, all of the buildings were demolished.

Description: Square brick tower

Location: Mark Island

Directions: Accessible by boat

Coordinates: 44°08'03.6"N 68°42'12.6"W

Opened: 1858

Automated: 1958

Deactivated: Active

Lens: Fourth-order Fresnel lens

Height: 25 feet

Focal Height: 52 feet

Signal: Flashing white every six seconds

Foghorn Signal: 1 blast every 15 seconds

Visitor Access: Grounds open, tower closed

Dice Head Lighthouse

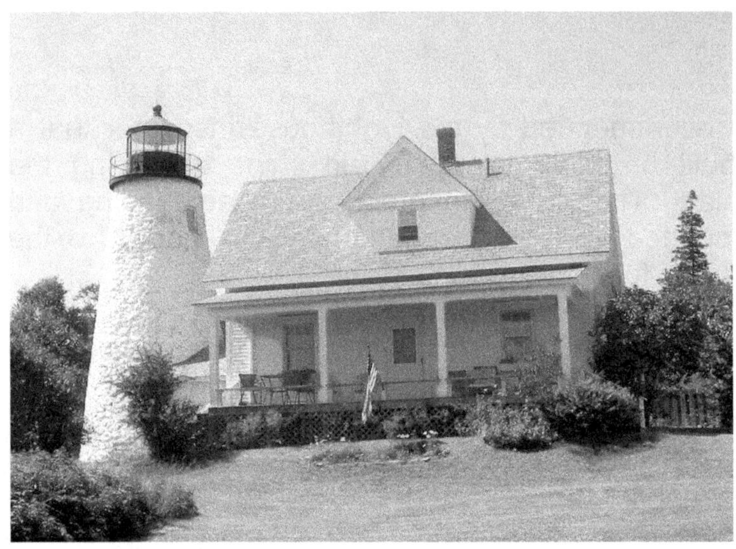

The Dice Head Lighthouse was opened in 1828 as a navigation aid for ships travelling the Penobscot River to enter the harbor at Castine.

The Dice Head Lighthouse was decommissioned in 1937 when the light was moved to a skeleton tower. However when the skeleton tower was destroyed in a storm, a light was installed in the old tower in 2008 and has been active since. The lighthouse was added to the National Register of Historic Places as part of the Castine Historic District on February 23, 1973.

Description: White tower

Location: Town of Castine

Directions: In Castine, head SW on Battle Ave from Castine Road for 1.2 mi and turn slightly right on Dyces Head Rd and the site is 0.1 mi

Coordinates: 44°22'58.3"N 68°49'08.4"W

Opened: 1828

Automated: 2008

Deactivated: 1937-2008 Reactivated in 2008

Height: 51 feet

Focal Height: 134 feet

Lens: Fourth-order Fresnel lens

Signal: White flash every 6 seconds

Visitor Access: Grounds open, tower closed

Doubling Point Range Lighthouses

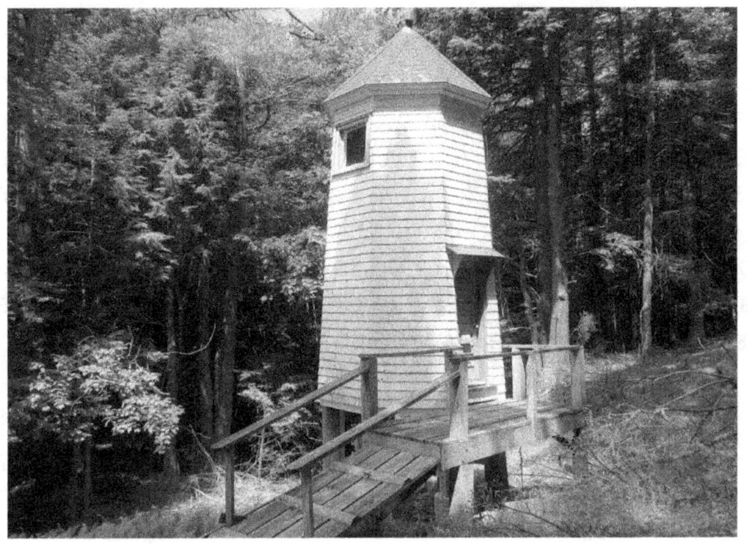

The Doubling Points on the Kennebec River refer to a section of the river where upstream ships encounter a 90° turn west followed by a 90° turn north. Two range lights were built in 1898 to aid ships to properly align themselves for these dangerous turns. Shortly thereafter a boat house and oil house were added to the station

A non-profit group, the Range Light Keepers restored the rear range tower in 2017, and the front tower in 2019.

	Doubling Point Front	**Doubling Point Rear**
Description:	Octagonal wood frame	Octagonal wood frame

Directions: Take Whitmore's Landing Rd. west from Highway 127 for 0.5 mi and take a sharp left onto Doubling Point Rd. for 0.1 mi where a path by a parking area will bring you to the Lights

Coordinates:	43°52'58.3"N 69°47'44.4"W	43°52'58.3"N 69°47'44.4"W
Opened:	1898	1898
Automated:	1988	1988
Deactivated:	Active	Active
Height:	18 feet	18 feet
Focal Height:	21 feet	33 feet
Signal:	White Quick Flashes	Iso White 6 seconds
Visitor Access:	Grounds open, tower closed	Grounds open, tower closed

Doubling Point Lighthouse

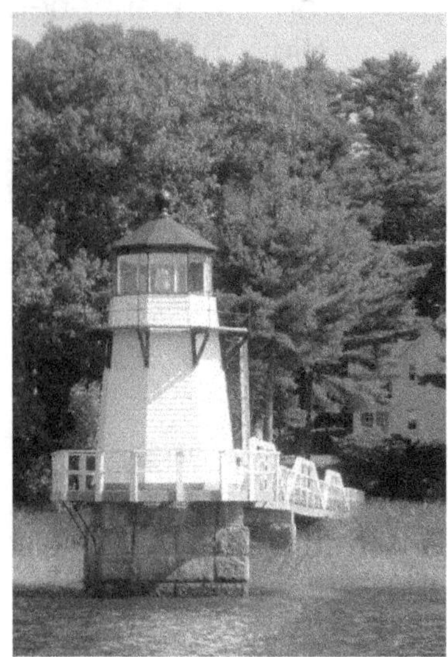

The Lighthouse Board proposed that 5 lights be built along the Kennebec River and Congress agreed. In 1898 the Doubling Point Lighthouse was opened along with the Doubling Point Range Lights, Perkins Island Light, and Squirrel Point Light. The tower was moved to its present location in 1899.
By 1999 the foundation had deteriorated to the point that the tower was endangered. The tower was moved temporarily while the foundation was repaired and the tower was returned early in 2000.

The light was listed on the National Register of Historic Places as Doubling Point Light Station on January 21, 1988.

Description: Octagonal Wood Tower

Location: Arrowsic Island

Directions: From Highway 1 on the east side of Kennebec River turn south on Highway 127 (Five Islands Road) and go 1.8 mi. Turn right onto Whitmore's Landing Road and continue 0.4 mi then turn left onto Doubling Point Road and the lighthouse is at the end

Coordinates: 43°52'57.1"N 69°48'24.2"W

Opened: 1898

Automated: 1988

Deactivated: Active

Lens: Fifth-order Fresnel lens

Height: 23 feet

Focal Height: 25 feet

Signal: White flash every 4 seconds

Visitor Access: Grounds open, tower closed

Eagle Island Lighthouse

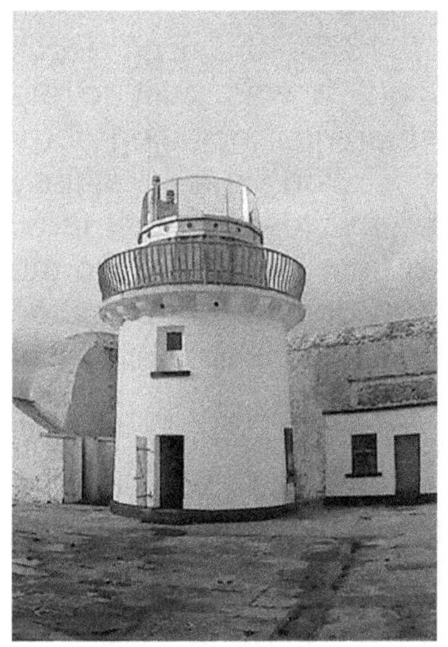

A lighthouse was needed for Eagle Island to protect shipping moving in and out of Bangor. The Eagle Island Lighthouse opened in 1838. However it soon ran into problems. In a 1842 report, the keeper, Nathan Philbrook, outlined the many defects he encountered due to poor workmanship. The tower leaked, the deck had heaved, and the light was ineffective due to a poor placement. The structure finally had to be rebuilt in 1858.

In 1963 all of the buildings but the lighthouse and bell tower were demolished by the coastguard.

Description: White conical tower

Location: Northeast tip of Eagle Island

Directions: Accessible by boat

Coordinates: 44°13'03.5"N 68°46'04.0"W

Opened: 1839

Automated: 1959

Deactivated: Active

Height: 30 feet

Focal Height: 106 feet

Lens: VLB-44

Signal: White flash every 4 seconds

Visitor Access: Grounds open, tower closed

Egg Rock Lighthouse

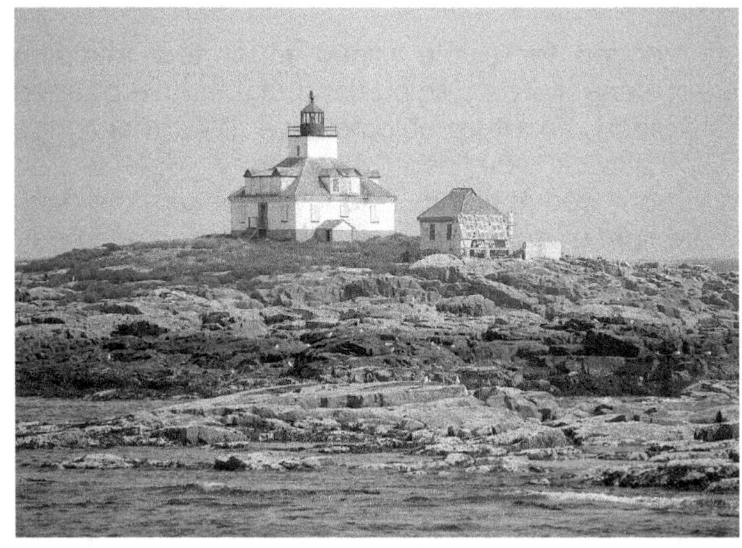

In November of 1875, the Egg Rock Lighthouse opened. It was built to aid navigation for shipping, including ferry services. The station was initially equipped with a fifth-order Fresnel lens. In 1899 a second floor was added to the dwelling which provided accommodation for an assistant keeper who had been hired in 1898.

The island received its name from the large numbers of sea birds who nested there. Unfortunately they abandoned the site after the lighthouse was built.

The site was listed by the National Register of Historic Places on January 21, 1988.

Description: Square tower

Location: Rock Island

Directions: Accessible by boat

Coordinates: 44°21'14.7"N 68°08'17.0"W

Opened: 1875

Automated: 1976

Deactivated: Active

Height: 39 feet

Focal Height: 64 feet

Lens: VRB-25

Signal: Red flash every 5 seconds

Foghorn Signal: 2 blasts every 30 seconds

Visitor Access: Grounds open, tower closed

Fort Point Lighthouse

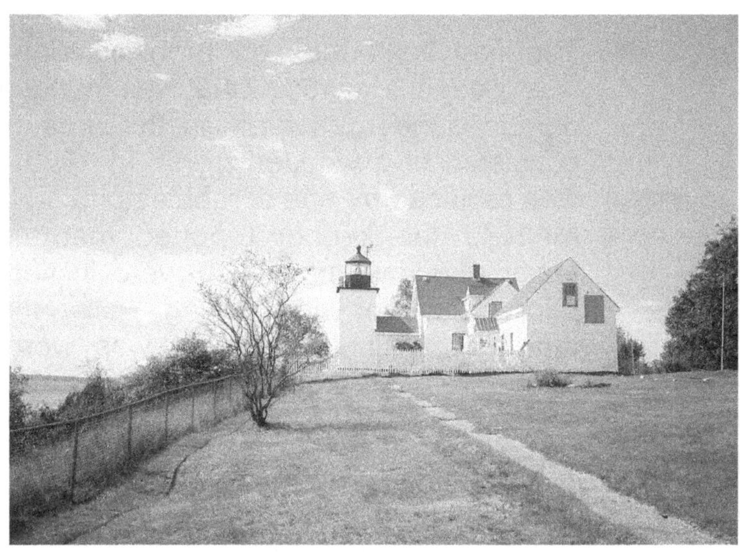

In 1834 Congress budgeted funds for a lighthouse at Fort Point to aid ships carrying lumber and potatoes. An inspection of the station in 1840 described serious problems including cracks in the tower walls and a leaking roof. It was years later before the decision was made to replace the tower and the new tower began operation in 1857.
In 1890 a bell tower was added as was an oil house in 1897.

Listed on the National Register of Historic Places on March 23, 1988.

Description: Square Brick Tower

Location: Fort Point State Park

Directions: From Highway 1 near Stockton Springs, take Main Street and turn south on Cape Jellison Road. After 0.8 miles, take the left fork for 1.6 miles to the park entrance. Take Lighthouse Road to the lighthouse.

Coordinates: 44°28'02.0"N 68°48'42.0"W

Opened: 1857

Automated: 1988

Deactivated: Active

Height: 31 feet

Focal Height: 88 feet

Lens: Fourth-order Fresnel lens

Signal: Flashing white

Foghorn Signal: 1 blast every 10 seconds

Visitor Access: Grounds open, tower closed

Franklin Island Lighthouse

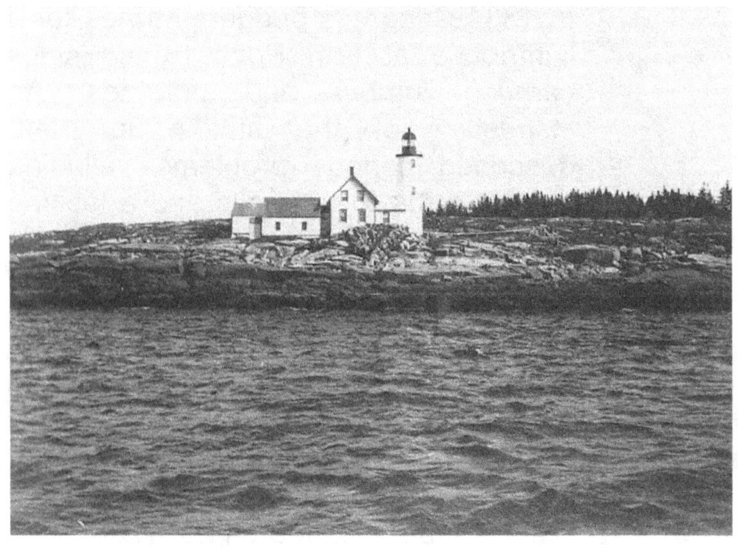

The first lighthouse on Franklin Island was opened in 1807 and was needed due to dangerous reefs in the area. It consisted of a wooden tower. In 1830 it was replaced by one of rubblestone.
In 1842 the keeper reported that the tower and dwelling house were in very poor condition with leaking walls and that the lighting equipment was worn. The lighthouse inspector recommended replacement and the current tower was lit in 1855.

Description: White tower

Location: Franklin Island

Directions: Accessible by boat

Coordinates: 43°53'32.0"N 69°22'29.4"W

Opened: 1855

Automated: 1933

Deactivated: Active

Height: 45 feet

Focal Height: 57 feet

Lens: VLB-44

Signal: White flash every 6 seconds

Visitor Access: Grounds open, tower closed

Goat Island Lighthouse

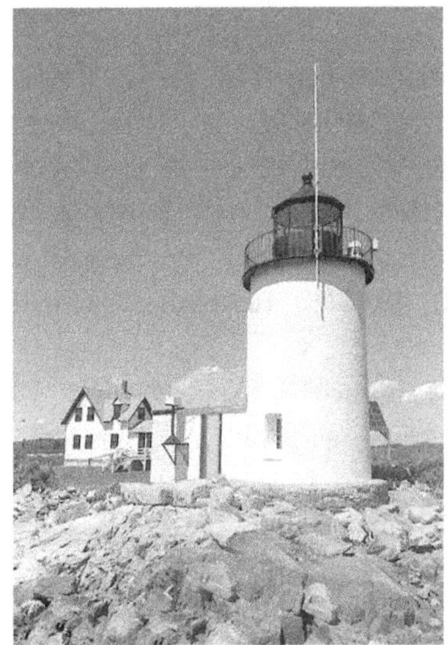

A lighthouse was built on Goat Island in 1833. An 1842 report of the lighthouse found it in poor condition, with leaking walls and roof, as well as rotting woodwork. A new tower was needed but it would not be built until 1859.

Listed on the National Register of Historic Places on March 23, 1988.

Description: White cylindrical tower

Location: Goat Island

Directions: Accessible by boat

Coordinates: 43°21'28.1"N 70°25'30.3"W

Opened: 1859

Automated: 1990

Deactivated: Active

Lens: VLB-44

Height: 25 feet

Focal Height: 38 feet

Signal: White flash every 6 seconds

Foghorn Signal: Blast every 15 seconds

Visitor Access: Grounds open, tower closed

Goose Rocks Lighthouse

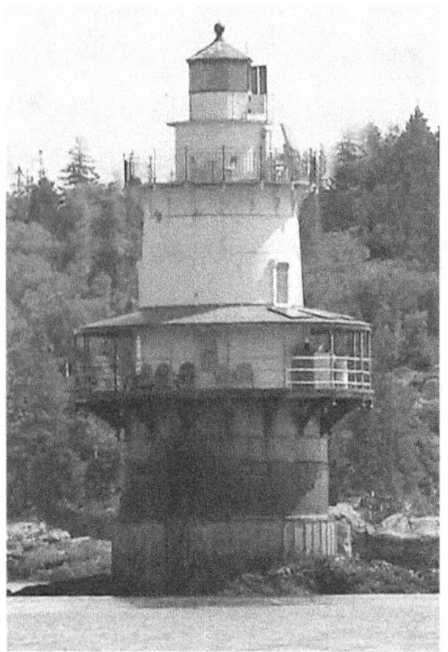

Congress budgeted funds for the Goose Rocks Lighthouse in 1888 and the lighthouse opened in 1890. An iron caisson twenty-five feet in diameter and and twenty-four feet high was anchored to the rock ledge and partially filled with concrete, while the tower itself was made up of three layers used for a dwelling, topped by a watch room and then the lantern room. Due to its structure, it is often referred to as a spark plug lighthouse.
Goose Rocks Lighthouse has been restored and is available to overnight visitors.

Listed to the National Register of Historic Places as Goose Rocks Light Station on January 21, 1988

Description: White conical tower

Location: Entrance to the Fox Islands Thoroughfare

Directions: Accessible by boat

Coordinates: 44°08'07.7"N 68°49'50.1"W

Opened: 1890

Automated: 1963

Deactivated: Active

Lens: 250 mm lens

Height: 51 feet

Focal Height: 51 feet

Signal: Red flash every 6 seconds

Foghorn Signal: 1 blast every 10 seconds

Visitor Access: Overnight stays are available

Great Duck Lighthouse

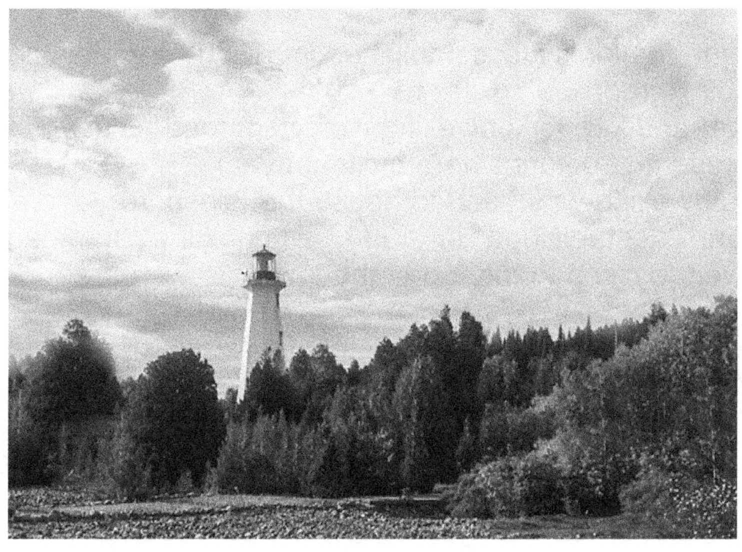

A Lighthouse has been requested to protect the entrance to Mount Desert harbor as well as Bass harbor as early as the 1840s. However it wasn't until 1890 before it was realized. At that time, a boathouse, a barn, a fog signal house, the 42 foot cylindrical brick tower and a dwelling for the keeper and his assistants were built. The Lighthouse was automated in 1986.
The station was listed in the National Register of Historic Places on March 14, 1988.

Description: White tower

Location: Great Duck Island

Directions: Accessible by boat

Coordinates: 44°08'32.0"N 68°14'45.1"W

Opened: 1890

Automated: 1986

Deactivated: Active

Height: 42 feet

Focal Height: 67 feet

Lens: VRB-25

Signal: Red flash every 5 seconds

Foghorn Signal: 2 second blast every 15 seconds

Visitor Access: Grounds closed, tower closed

Grindle Point Lighthouse

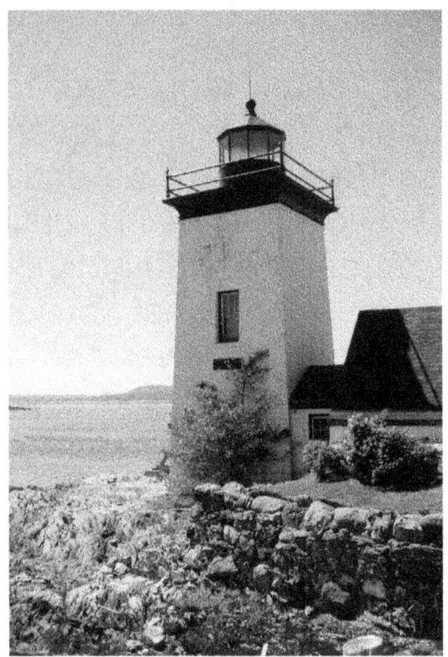

The Grindle Point Station was established in 1850 to mark the entrance to Gilkey Harbor.
By 1874 the tower and keeper's dwelling were regarded as beyond repair and the present structures were built that year.
The old keeper's dwelling was used to house the Islesboro Sailors' Memorial Museum, established in 1938. During the summer, visitors are allowed to climb to the top of the tower.

The station is listed in the National Register of Historic Places on March 13, 1987

Description: Square white tower

Location: Islesboro Island

Directions: 615 Ferry Rd, Islesboro

Coordinates: 44°16'53.3"N 68°56'34.7"W

Opened: 1874

Automated: 1987

Deactivated: Deactivated 1934 Reactivated 1987

Lens: VLB-44

Height: 39 feet

Focal Height: 39 feet

Signal: White flash every 4 seconds

Visitor Access: Grounds open, tower open in summer

Halfway Rock Lighthouse

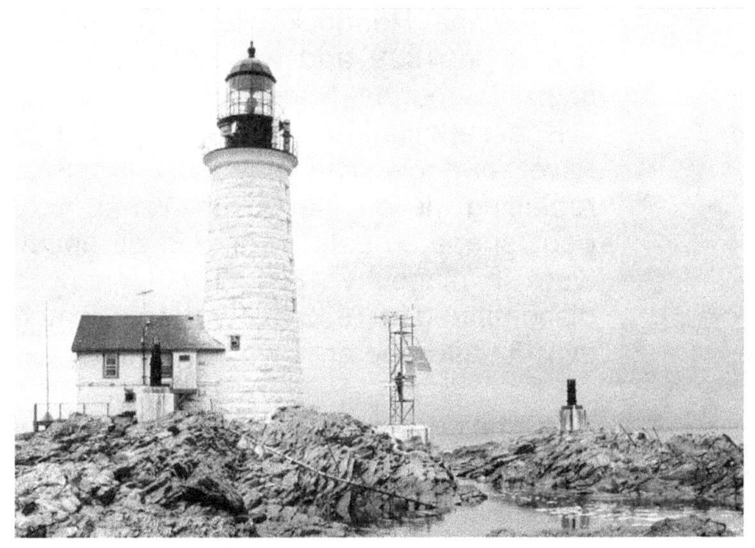

Halfway Rock is situated in Canso Bay and requests for a lighthouse were made as early as 1835. However decades would pass, while ships and lives were lost, before Congress budgeted funds for a lighthouse. The Halfway Rock Lighthouse finally opened in 1871. A bell tower was added to the station in 1887 and this was upgraded to a diesel-powered Daboll foghorn in 1905. In 1889 a boathouse was built and an oil house in 1890.

The station was automated in 1975.

Halfway Rock Light was added to the National Register of Historic Places as Halfway Rock Light Station on March 14, 1988.

Description: White tower attached to dwelling

Location: Halfway Rock

Directions: Accessible by boat

Coordinates: 43°39'20.9"N 70°02'12.8"W

Opened: 1871

Automated: 1975

Deactivated: Active

Height: 76 feet

Focal Height: 77 feet

Lens: VRB-25

Signal: Red flash every 5 seconds

Foghorn Signal: 2 blasts every 30 seconds

Visitor Access: Grounds and tower closed

Hendricks Head Lighthouse

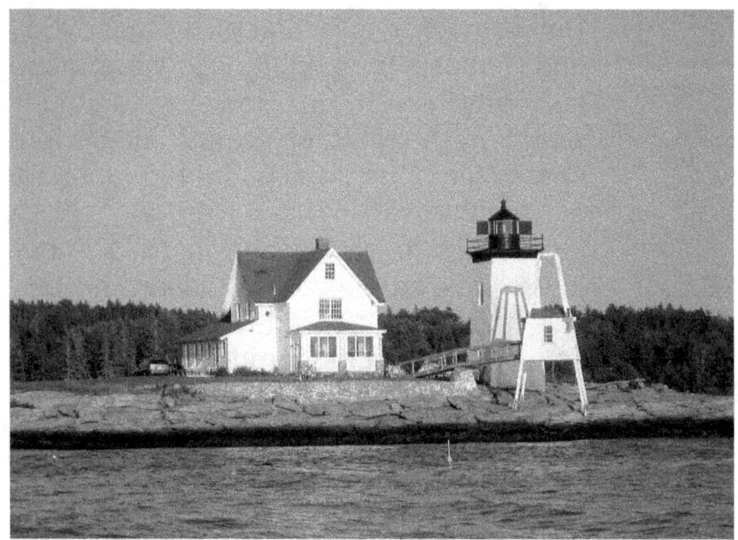

The original Hendricks Head Lighthouse was lit in 1829 and was built to guide ships through Sheepscot River to Wiscasset Harbor. A new lighthouse tower and dwelling was built in 1875, replacing the original which was in very poor shape. A bell tower and oil house were in place by 1891. The Light was discontinued in 1933 but was reactivated in 1951 after the area was electrified.

The station was listed on the National Register of Historic Places on November 20, 1987.

Description: Square Brick Tower

Location: Southport Island

Directions: Accessible by boat

Coordinates: 43°49'21.3"N 69°41'23.0"W

Opened: 1875

Automated: 1951

Deactivated: Deactivated in 1933, reactivated in 1951

Height: 39 feet

Focal Height: 43 feet

Lens: 250mm lens

Signal: Continuous white to the west and red to the east

Visitor Access: Grounds and tower closed

Heron Neck Lighthouse

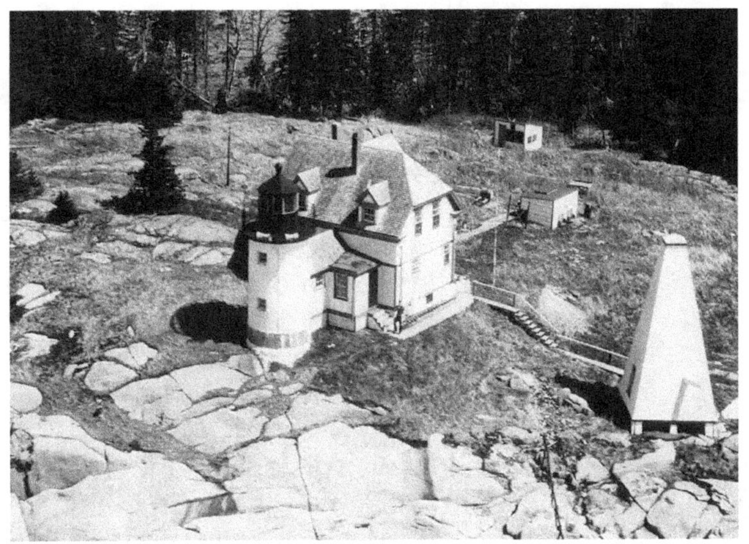

Heron Neck Light was established in 1854 to guide shipping to the town of Vinalhaven's main port and the Hurricane Channel to the northwest. The Lighthouse Board report in 1891 found the keeper's dwelling in poor condition with the walls becoming damp in storms and the cellar wet. It was replaced by the current building in 1895. An oil house was added in 1903 and a boathouse in 1904.

The station was automated in 1982 and a 300mm lens replaced the fourth-order Fresnel lens.

Heron Neck Light was listed on National Register of Historic Places on January 21, 1988

Description: White conical tower

Location: Green Island

Directions: Accessible by boat

Coordinates: 44°01'30.9"N 68°51'42.8"W

Opened: 1854

Automated: 1982

Deactivated: Active

Height: 30 feet

Focal Height: 92 feet

Lens: 300mm lens

Signal: Fixed red with white sector

Foghorn Signal: 1 blast every 30 seconds

Visitor Access: Grounds and tower closed

Indian Island Lighthouse

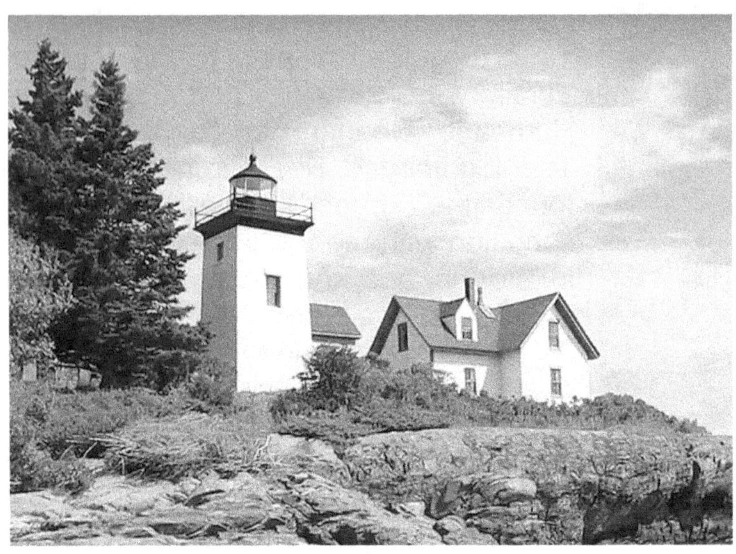

The station at Indian Island was first serviced by a lantern on the roof of the dwelling from 1850. The light was deactivated in 1859 as it was thought to be unnecessary. In 1875 it was re-lit with a new lighthouse tower and repairs to the dwelling house.
In 1902 a fourth-order Fresnel lens replaced the fifth-order Fresnel lens and in 1904 an oil house was built. The station was automated in 1949.

The station was listed on the National Register of Historic Places on March 23, 1988

Description: Square Brick Tower

Location: Indian Island

Directions: Accessible by boat

Coordinates: 44°09'55.7"N 69°03'39.5"W

Opened: 1875

Automated: 1949

Deactivated: 1859-1874, presently active

Height: 31 feet

Lens: Fourth-order Fresnel lens

Visitor Access: Grounds and tower closed

Note: Privately owned

Isle au Haut Lighthouse

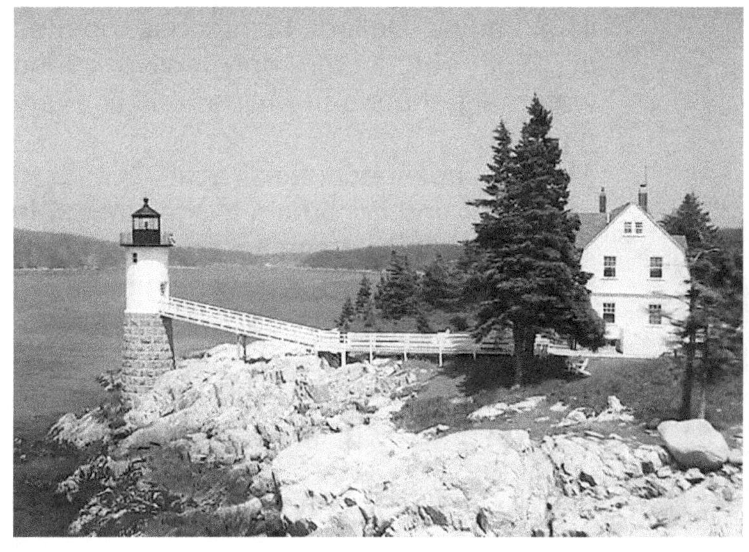

Lower East Penobscot Bay is a productive fishing grounds and the Isle au Haut Lighthouse was opened in 1907 as an aid to the many vessels engaged there. The station also includes a large Keeper's dwelling, a boathouse, storage building and an oil house. The station was automated in 1933. After automation, the fourth-order Fresnel lens was replaced by a a fifth-order Fresnel lens, and eventually to a 250mm lens. Substantial restoration work was performed between 2016 and 2021. Listed with the National Register of Historic Places on January 21, 1988.

Description: White conical tower

Location: Isle au Haut

Directions: Take the ferry to Isle au Haut from Stonington, Connecticut

Coordinates: 44°03'53.1"N 68°39'05.0"W

Opened: 1907

Automated: 1934

Deactivated: Active

Height: 40 feet

Focal Height: 47 feet

Lens: 250mm lens

Signal: Red flash every 3 seconds with white sector

Foghorn Signal: Discontinued in 1934

Visitor Access: Grounds open, tower closed. The Keeper's House is available to rent

Ladies Delight Lighthouse

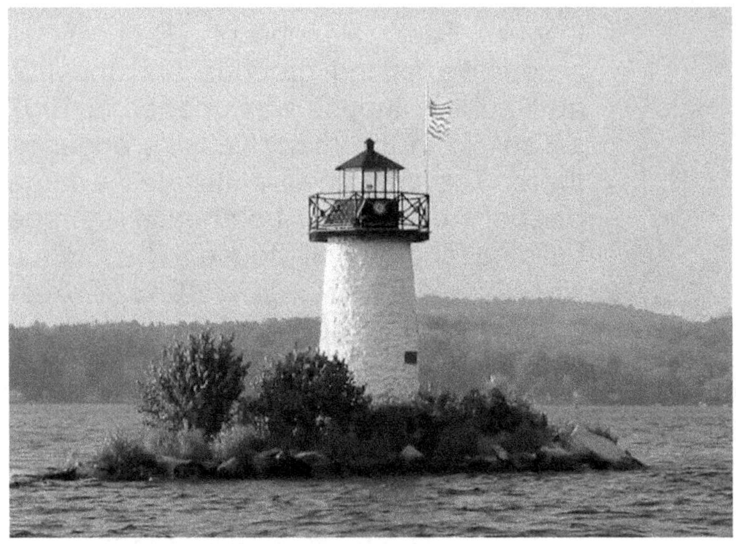

The Ladies Delight Lighthouse opened in 1908 and is the only active inland waters lighthouse in Maine. It is lit every night.
The Cobbosseecontee Yacht Club built the tower and continues to maintain it. In 2005 work was done to correct a lean that had developed. A new aluminum top was constructed in 2005.

The Ladies Delight Light was listed on the National Register of Historic Places in January 12, 1984.

Description: Conical brick tower

Location: Lake Cobbosseecontee

Directions: Best seen by boat, distant views from shore

Coordinates: 44°18'16.0"N 69°53'47.9"W

Opened: 1908

Automated: 1908

Deactivated: Active

Height: 16 feet

Lens: Solar powered dual-level LED marine beacon

Visitor Access: Grounds and tower closed

Libby Island Lighthouse

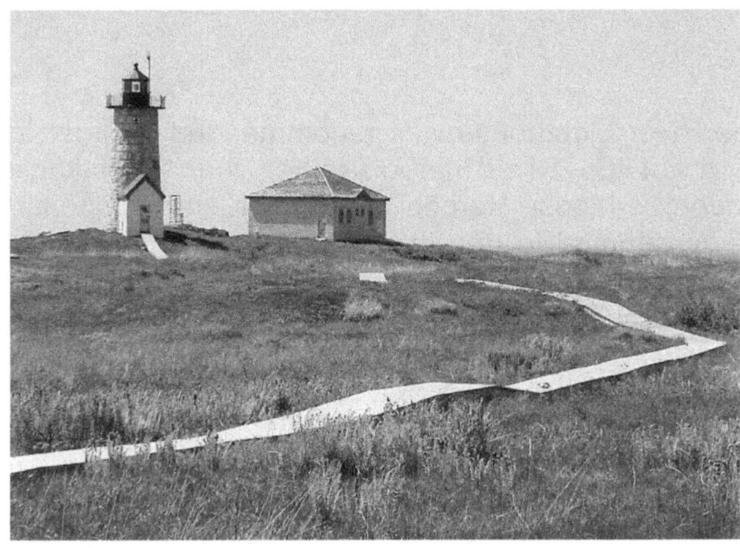

In 1822 a tower was opened on Libby Island but it soon developed cracks and collapsed in 6 months. The tower was rebuilt and made active in 1823. A Keeper's dwelling was added in 1824 but by 1850 it was reported to be in very bad condition. A new dwelling was built in 1854.

It is listed on the National Register of Historic Places as Libby Island Light Station on June 18, 1976.

Description: White Tower

Location: Libby Island

Directions: Accessible by boat

Coordinates: 44°34'05.8"N 67°22'02.4"W

Opened: 1823

Automated: 1974

Deactivated: Active

Height: 42 feet

Focal Height: 91 feet

Lens: VRB-25

Signal: Double white flash every 20 seconds

Foghorn Signal: 1 blast every 15 seconds

Visitor Access: Grounds and tower closed

Little River Lighthouse

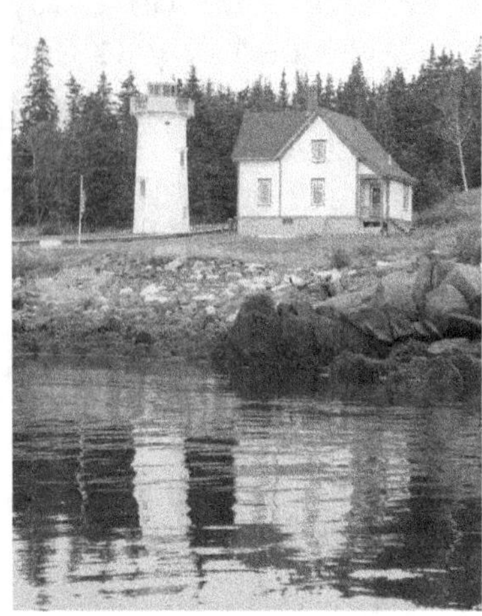

In 1942 the Little River Lighthouse was recommended in order to guide ships to the Little River harbor rather than mistakenly entering the dangerous Moose Harbor. In 1848 the station opened but by 1876 it was deemed to be beyond repairing. A new tower was built that year. In 1888 the original dwelling was demolished and a new house was built.

The lighthouse is listed on the National Register of Historic Places on March 14, 1988.

Description: Cylindrical Cast Iron Tower

Location: Little River Island

Directions: Accessible by boat

Coordinates: 44°39'03.1"N 67°11'32.4"W

Opened: 1876

Automated: 1975

Deactivated: Deactivated from 1975-2001 when Reactivated

Lens: VRB-25

Height: 41 feet

Focal Height: 56 feet

Signal: White flash every 6 seconds

Foghorn Signal: 1 blast every 10 seconds

Visitor Access: Grounds are open June–October, tower open during open house

Lubec Channel Lighthouse

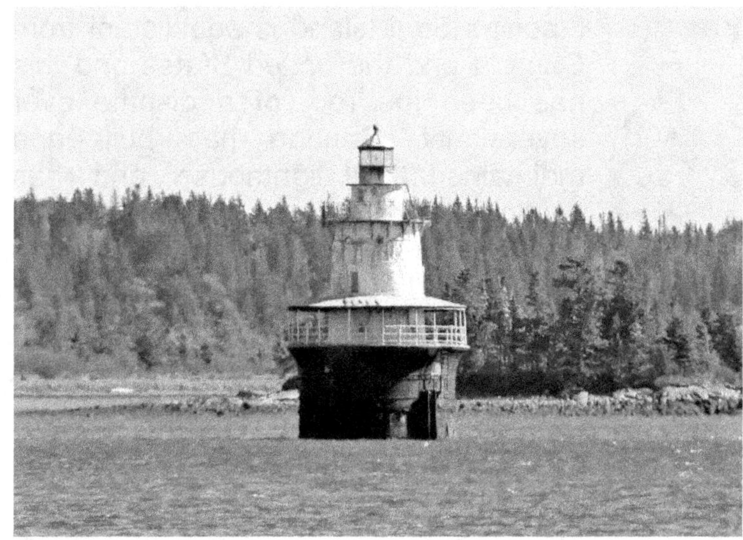

Due to its shape, the Lubec Channel Light is often termed a sparkplug lighthouse, one of three in the state. It was opened in 1890 as an aid to navigation on the Bay of Fundy route to Eastport, Maine and is only 500 feet from the Canadian border.

The light was built on an iron caisson which was filled with concrete. The light opened in 1890, equipped with a fifth-order Fresnel lens.

In 1992, an expensive renovation corrected a lean which had developed. The station is listed with the National Register of Historic Places on March 14, 1988.

Description: White conical tower on black cylindrical pier

Location: Lubec Channel

Directions: From Highway 1 in Whiting, go east on Highway 189 for 10 miles, then turn south on Boot Cove Road where there is a distant view of the lighthouse

Coordinates: 44°50'31.4"N 66°58'35.8"W

Opened: 1890

Automated: 1939

Deactivated: Active

Height: 39 feet

Focal Height: 53 feet

Lens: VLB-44

Signal: White flash every 6 seconds

Foghorn Signal: 2 second blast every 15 seconds

Visitor Access: Grounds and tower closed

Machias Seal Island Lighthouse

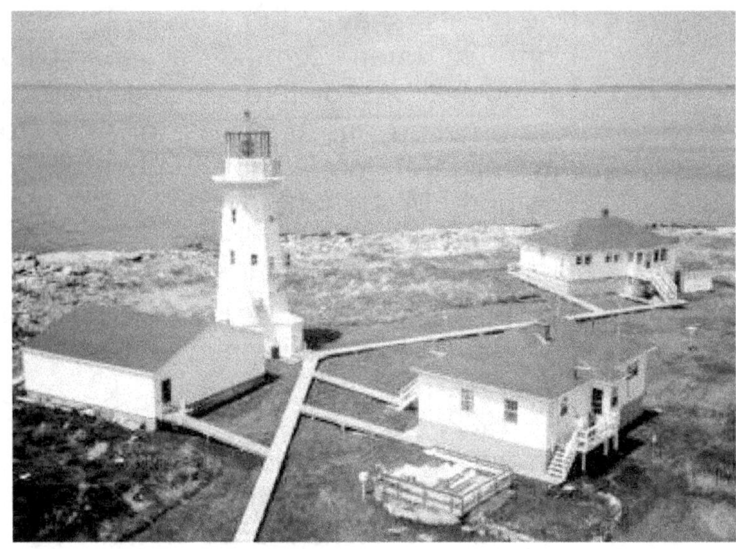

Machias Seal Island is equidistant from Canada and the united States and this has been the root of a dispute over sovereignty. Canada has built and maintained the lighthouse and has continued to staff it with keepers, as well as as a warden to regulates visitors who come to see puffins. As this is a prime fishing grounds, the United States continues to maintain its sovereignty as well.

In 1832 two wooden towers were built on the island. As the area is often in fog, a signal gun was added in 1841. In 1856-1857, the station underwent repairs to both the towers and dwelling. A replacement for one of the towers opened in 1878 and a fog alarm was added in 1914. The current tower replaced the two existing in 1915.

Description: Tapered octagonal tower

Location: Machias Seal Island

Directions: Accessible by boat

Coordinates: 44°30'06.6"N 67°06'04.1"W

Opened: 1915

Automated: Not automated

Deactivated: Active

Height: 60 feet

Signal: Flashing white

Foghorn Signal: One 2 second blast every 15 seconds

Visitor Access: Grounds open, tower closed

Marshall Point Lighthouse

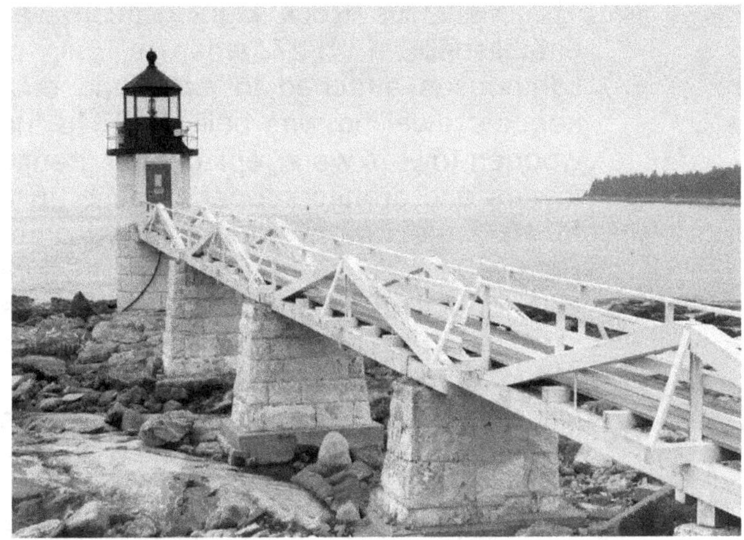

The first Marshall Point Lighthouse was opened in 1832. it was a twenty foot conical tower with a dwelling built at the same time.

By 1942 the keeper was reporting that the station was in very bad condition with the joints leaking and causing ice in the structures in winter.

The present tower was constructed in 1857 and was equipped with a fifth-order Fresnel lens with a fixed white light. In 1891 a fuel house was built and the next year a boathouse was added. In March 2017, the Coast Guard upgraded the light with a modern LED.

Listed in the National Register of Historic Places March 23, 1988

Description: White cylindrical tower

Location: Entrance to Port Clyde

Directions: From Highway 1 east of Thomason, turn south on Highway 131 and continue for 13.6 miles. Turn left on Drift Inn Road and then right on Marshall Point Road. Follow Marshall Point Road for a mile to its end at the lighthouse parking

Coordinates: 43°55'02.7"N 69°15'40.6"W

Opened: 1857

Automated: 1971

Deactivated: Active

Height: 30 feet

Focal Height: 31 feet

Lens: VLB-44

Signal: Fixed white

Foghorn Signal: 1 second blast every 10 seconds

Visitor Access: Grounds open, tower closed

Matinicus Rock Lighthouse

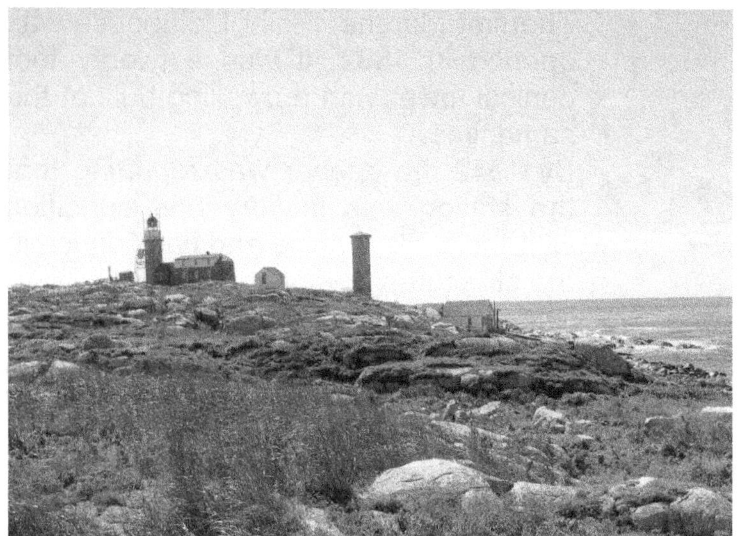

The Matinicus Rock Light Station was established in 1827 when a pair of lighthouses attached to each end of a keepers dwelling was built. In 1846 the wooden towers were replaced by granite towers and granite keeper's house built. In 1857 the towers received third order Fresnel lenses. In 1924 the north light was deactivated and the station was changed to a single tower.

Abbie Burgess, a daughter of a keeper, twice operated the station for weeks when her father, who had gone to shore, could not get back due to storms.

The lighthouse was added to the National Register of Historic Places as Matinicus Rock Light Station on March 14, 1988.

Description: Cylindrical gray granite tower

Location: Matinicus Rock

Directions: Accessible by boat

Coordinates: 43°47'00.5"N 68°51'18.1"W

Opened: 1846

Automated: 1983

Deactivated: Active

Height: 48 feet

Focal Height: 90 feet

Lens: VRB-25

Signal: White flash every 10 seconds

Foghorn Signal: One 2 second blast every 15 seconds

Visitor Access: Grounds and tower closed

Monhegan Island Lighthouse

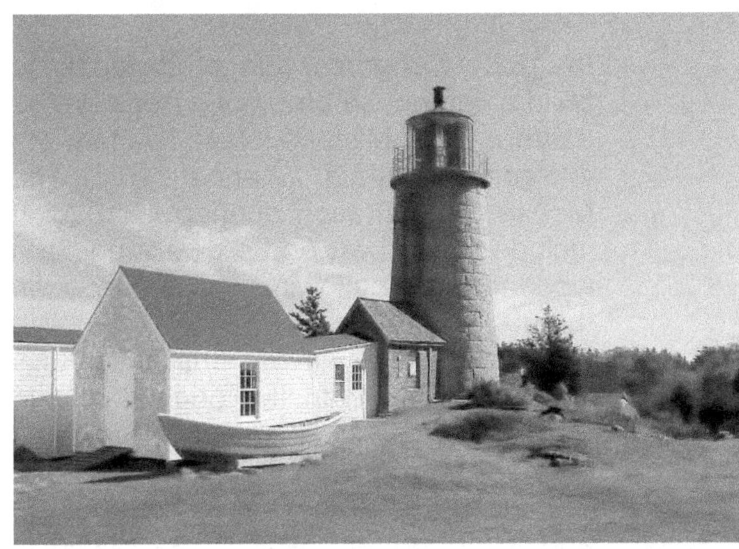

In 1822 Congress budgeted funds for a lighthouse on Monhegan Island and in 1824 the station was opened. In 1850 the stone tower was replaced by the current one of granite blocks. In 1857 the light was upgraded with a second-order Fresnel lens.

In 1959 the light was automated and in 1962 a museum was established in the vacant keeper's dwelling.

The station was listed in the National Register of Historic Places on May 07, 1980

Description: Granite tower

Location: Monhegan Island

Directions: Ferry from Port Clyde

Coordinates: 43°45'53.4"N 69°18'56.9"W

Opened: 1850

Automated: 1959

Deactivated: Active

Height: 47 feet

Focal Height: 178 feet

Lens: VRB-25

Signal: White flash every 15 seconds

Foghorn Signal: Separate fog station located on nearby Manana Island

Visitor Access: Grounds open, tower closed

Moose Peak (Mistake Island) Lighthouse

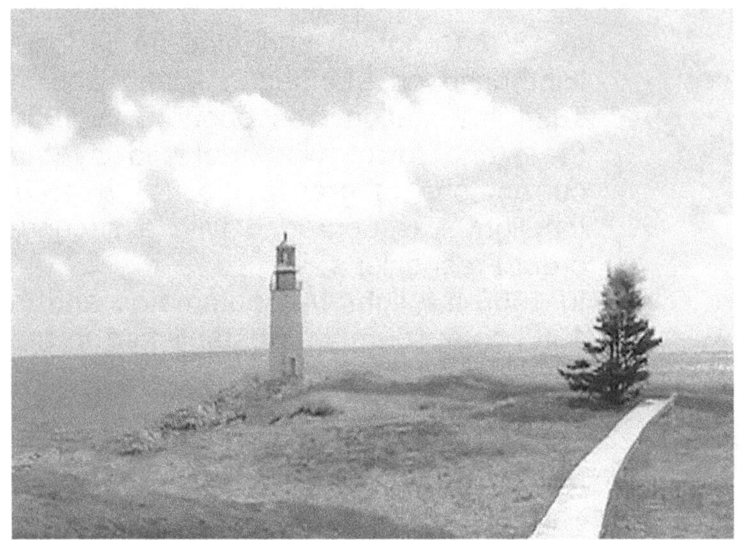

In 1825 Congress budgeted funds to build a lighthouse on Moose Peak on the eastern tip of Mistake Island to mark the entrance to Main Channel Way. The Moose Peak Station opened in 1826. It included the tower and a dwelling with a wooden bridge allowing access between them.

In 1851 a new tower was built which was 12 feet higher than the original and in 1854, a new keeper's dwelling was erected.

The area experiences many hours of fog and a fog signal building was raised in 1913.

Description: Conical brick tower

Location: Mistake Island

Directions: Accessible by boat

Coordinates: 44°28'28.5"N 67°31'55.2"W

Opened: 1851

Automated: 1972

Deactivated: Active

Height: 57 feet

Focal Height: 72 feet

Lens: VRB-25

Signal: White flash every 30 seconds

Foghorn Signal: 2 blasts every 30 seconds

Visitor Access: Grounds open, tower closed

Mount Desert Rock Lighthouse

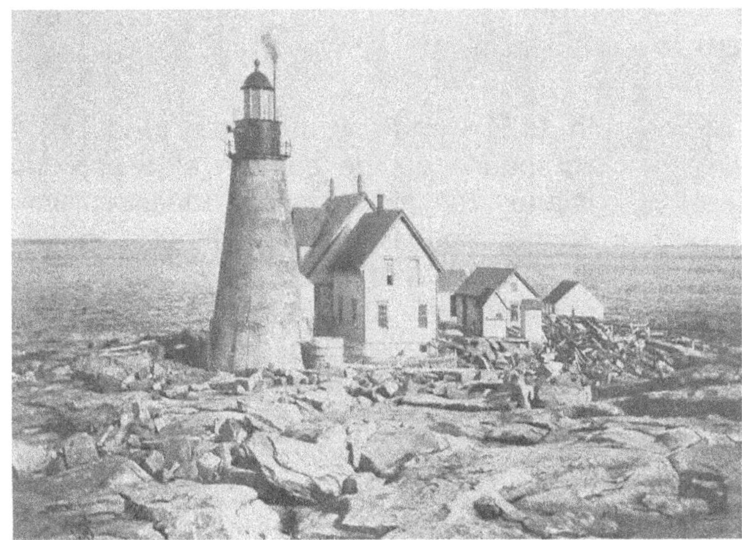

The first lighthouse on Mount Desert Rock opened in 1830. Mount Desert Rock is a small isolated islet far from the coast. As the rock itself is not much above the sea, it can be badly battered in a storm.

In just a year, the lighthouse was found to be in very poor shape with the joints leaking. In 1847 the present tower made of heavy granite blocks was opened. A third-order Fresnel lens was installed in 1857. In the 1850s a fog bell was added to the station along with an assistant to operate it. It was automated in 1977. It was listed on the National Register of Historic Places as Mount Desert Light Station in 1988.

Description: White conical tower

Location: Mount Desert Rock

Directions: Accessible by boat

Coordinates: 43°58'07.0"N 68°07'42.0"W

Opened: 1847

Automated: 1977

Deactivated: Active

Height: 58 feet

Focal Height: 75 feet

Lens: VLB-44

Signal: White flash every 15 seconds

Foghorn Signal: 2 blasts every 30 seconds

Visitor Access: Grounds and tower closed

Narraguagus (Pond Island) Lighthouse

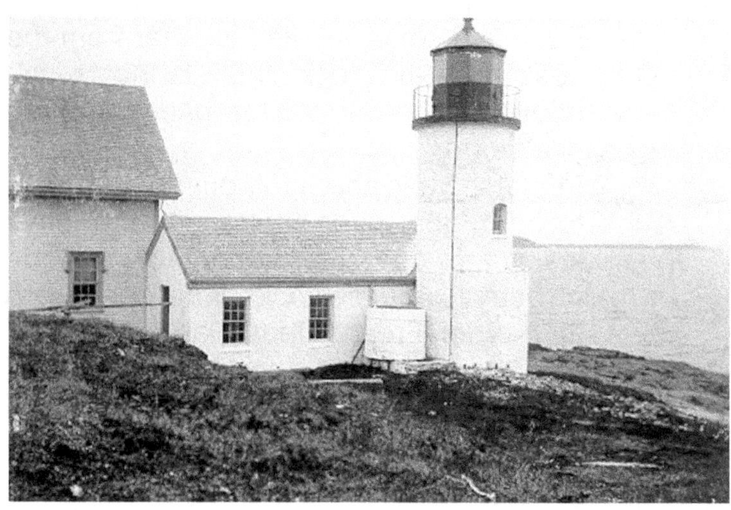

In 1851 Congress budgeted funds for a lighthouse on the eastern side of Pond Island to aid vessels passing into Narraguagus Bay and the station opened in 1853. A fifth-order Fresnel lens upgraded the light in 1856. The original keeper's dwelling was replaced in 1875 and a new deck and lantern were done at the same time. A fog bell was added as well.

The station was deactivated in 1933 and sold into private hands the following year.

It was listed on the National Register of Historic Places as "Narraguagus Light Station" on November 20, 1987.

Description: White tower

Location: Pond Island

Directions: Accessible by boat

Coordinates: 44°27'21.6"N 67°49'52.4"W

Opened: 1853

Automated: 1929

Deactivated: 1934

Height: 31 feet

Focal Height: 52 feet

Signal: White flash every 6 seconds

Foghorn Signal: 2 blasts every 30 seconds

Visitor Access: Grounds and tower closed, privately owned

Nash Island Lighthouse

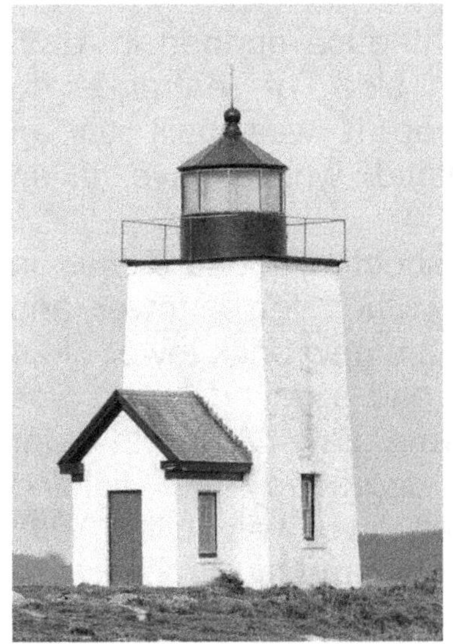

The first lighthouse was built on Nash Island in 1838 as an aid to shipping to the entrance of Moosabec Reach. It was a 24 foot tower built on a natural ledge with a keeper's dwelling. it was upgraded with a Fresnel lens in 1856.

The present square brick tower was erected in 1873. It is 35 feet high. A boathouse was added to the station in 1878 and in 1887 a fog tower was added.

The lighthouse was automated in 1947 and deactivated in 1982.

Description: Square white tower

Location: Nash Island

Directions: Accessible by boat

Coordinates: 44°27'51.5"N 67°44'50.2"W

Opened: 1873

Automated: 1947

Deactivated: 1982

Lens: Forth-order Fresnel lens

Height: 36 feet

Focal Height: 51 feet

Signal: White flash every 10 seconds

Foghorn Signal: Single and double blow at 20 second intervals

Visitor Access: Grounds open September-May, tower closed

Owls Head Lighthouse

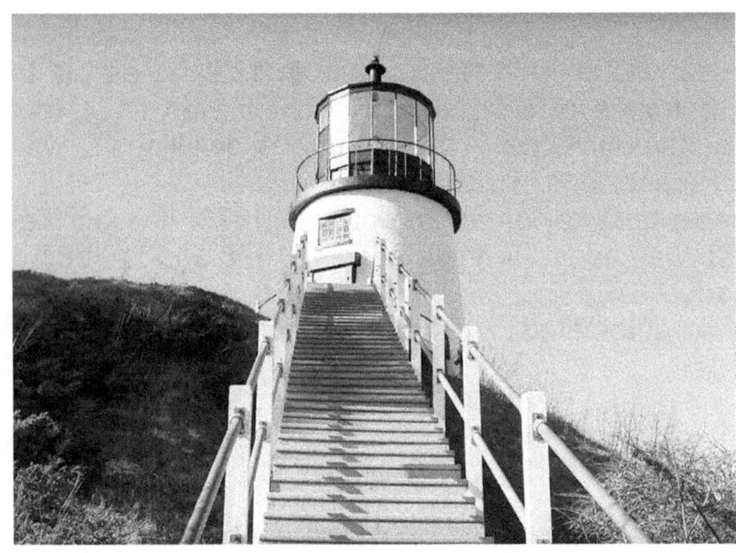

Owls Head Lighthouse opened in 1825 on the south side of entrance to Rockland Harbor. It was built on an elevated headland which gave it an extended range.

By 1842 an inspection found it was in poor condition with a leaky tower and dwelling. In 1852 a new brick tower of 24 feet replaced it and a new dwelling was built at the same time. A fourth-order Fresnel lens upgraded the lighting equipment. A bell tower was built in 1902 with up to date equipment.

The station was added to the National Register of Historic Places as Owls Head Light Station on January 18, 1978.

Description: White tower

Location: Entrance to Rockland Harbor

Directions: In Owls Head, turn left onto Main St and then left onto Lighthouse Rd, which leads the last 1.8 miles to Owls Head State Park and the lighthouse.

Coordinates: 44°05'32.1"N 69°02'38.7"W

Opened: 1852

Automated: 1989

Deactivated: Active

Height: 30 feet

Focal Height: 100 feet

Lens: Forth order Fresnel lens

Signal: Fixed white

Foghorn Signal: 2 blasts every 20 seconds

Visitor Access: Wednesdays from Memorial Day weekend to Columbus Day

Pemaquid Point Lighthouse

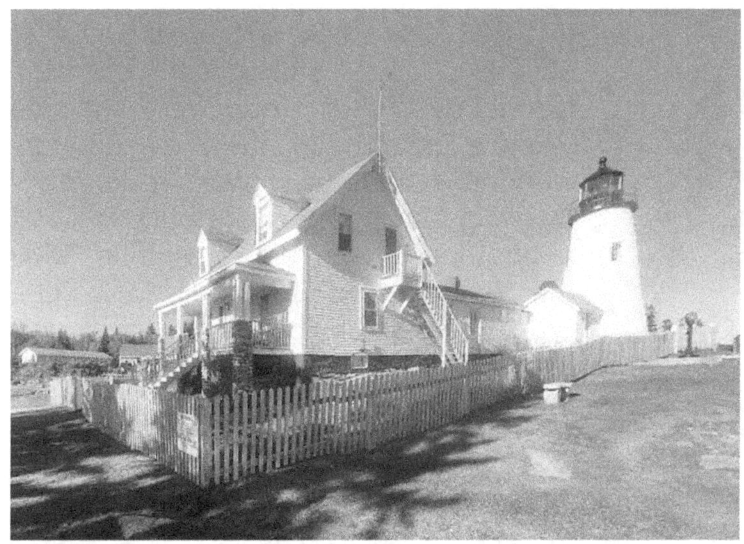

In 1827 the original lighthouse was built at Pemaquid Point showing a fixed white light. The station included a dwelling house with an attached kitchen. However it was replaced only 8 years later due to faults with the original structure. Part of the problems would seem to have been caused by the use of mortar mixed with sea water as this was specifically banned in the contract.

A fourth-order Fresnel lens was installed in 1857 and a new keeper's dwelling built at the same time. In 1899 a bell tower was added.

The station was listed with the National Register of Historic Places on April 16, 1985.

Description: White conical tower

Location: Tip of the Pemaquid Neck

Directions: From the Highway 1 in Damariscotta turn south on Highway 129 and drive for 2.9 mi and take Highway 130 south for 11.7 miles to the lighthouse.

Coordinates: 43°50'13.1"N 69°30'21.8"W

Opened: 1835

Automated: 1934

Deactivated: Active

Height: 38 feet

Focal Height: 79 feet

Lens: Fourth order Fresnel lens

Signal: White flash every 6 seconds

Visitor Access: Grounds and tower open mid-May through Columbus Day

Perkins Island Lighthouse

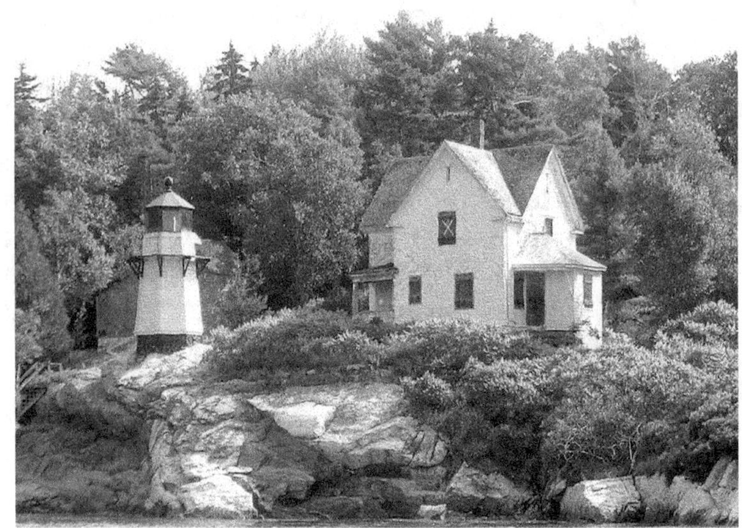

In 1895 Congress budgeted funds to establish 5 lighthouses on the Kennebec River including one on Perkins Island. In 1898 a 23 foot wooden octagonal tower, a keeper's dwelling and a barn were built. In 1901 a boathouse was added and in 1902 the lighting was upgraded to a fifth-order Fresnel lens and a bell tower was added. An oil house was added shortly thereafter.

In 1959 the station was automated, with the station still active today. In 2014 volunteers raised funds and provided their time to restore the dwelling. Listed on the National Register of Historic Places on January 21, 1988.

Description: Wooden octagonal tower

Location: Perkins Island

Directions: Accessible by boat

Coordinates: 43°47'12.9"N 69°47'06.1"W

Opened: 1898

Automated: 1959

Deactivated: Active

Height: 23 feet

Focal Height: 41 feet

Lens: 250mm lens

Signal: Red flash every 2.5 seconds and two white sectors

Visitor Access: Grounds open, tower closed

Petit Manan Lighthouse

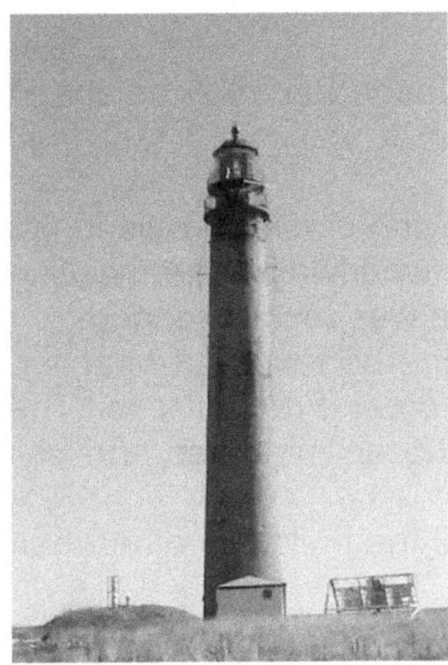

A small lighthouse was opened on Petit Manan Island in 1817. The Island has a colony of Puffins breeding there and is closed to visitors during breeding season. An 1831 report on the station noted it was in poor shape and included that the dwelling leaked badly. An 1842 report said that the tower walls and windows were cracked.
A new tower of granite blocks and a new keeper's dwelling were built in 1855. The tower is 119 feet high making it the second highest in Maine. The tower was equipped with a second-order Fresnel lens. A fog bell was added to the station in in 1853.

The station was listed on the National Register of Historic Places on October 30, 1987.

Description: Gray granite tower

Location: Petit Manan Island

Directions: Accessible by boat

Coordinates: 44°22'03.4"N 67°51'50.9"W

Opened: 1855

Automated: 1972

Deactivated: Active

Lens: VRB-25

Height: 119 feet

Focal Height: 123 feet

Signal: White flash every 10 seconds

Foghorn Signal: 1 blast every 30 seconds

Visitor Access: Grounds open September-March, tower closed

Pond Island Lighthouse

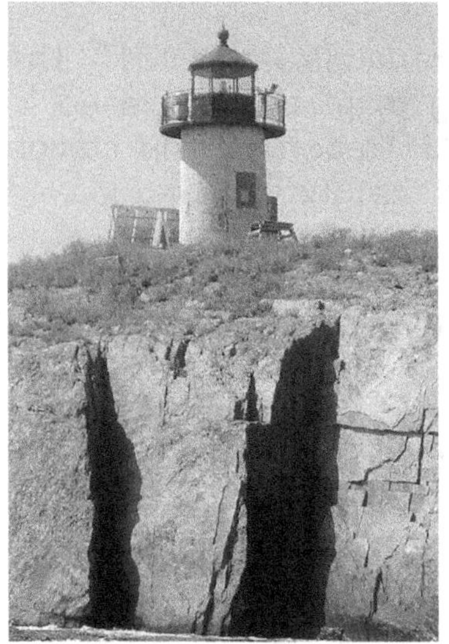

The first lighthouse on Pond island was opened in 1821 as an aid to shipping entering the Kennebec River. It was a 13 feet high tower.

In an 1842 report, it was described as having cracked walls in the tower as well as a leaky roof and rotting woodwork. The dwelling was also in poor condition. A new structure was recommended.

The current 20 foot brick tower opened in 1855 with an attached keeper's dwelling. It was lit with a fifth-order Fresnel lens. The station also included a fuel house. In 1905 an oil house and bell house were added.

In 1960 the station was automated and all the buildings other than the tower were demolished.

Description: White tower

Location: Pond Island

Directions: Accessible by boat

Coordinates: 43°44'24.0"N 69°46'13.0"W

Opened: 1855

Automated: 1960

Deactivated: Active

Lens: 250mm lens

Height: 20 feet

Focal Height: 52 feet

Signal: White flash every 6 seconds

Foghorn Signal: 2 blasts every 30 seconds

Visitor Access: Grounds open September-March, tower closed

Portland Breakwater Lighthouse

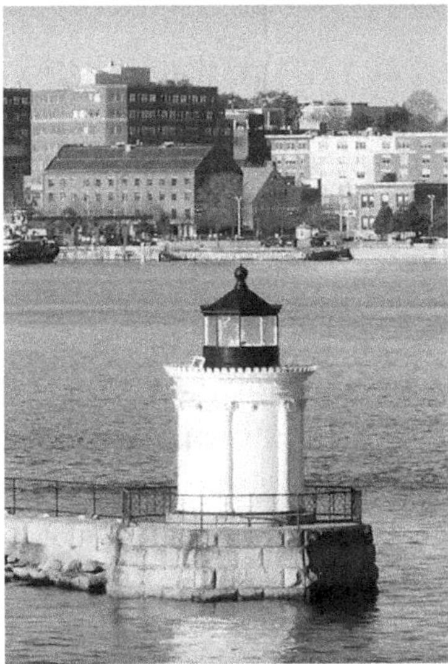

After a storm caused damage to ships and buildings in Portland Harbor in 1831, a breakwater was built by the entrance. The original plans called for a light at the end but it was not built at this time to to cost overruns. it wasn't until 1855 that an octagonal wooden tower was completed. A fixed red light shone from a sixth-order Fresnel lens to guide ships into the harbor.

The keeper's dwelling was replaced in 1871. The breakwater was extended in 1873 and the light was moved to the end of it.

In 1875 a 26 foot lighthouse of cast iron replaced the wooden structure and in 1903 a keeper's dwelling was attached to it. A fog bell was attached to it in 1898.

The light was automated in 1934 and the dwelling was removed at that time.

The station is listed on the National Register of Historic Places on June 19, 1973.

Description: White tower

Location: South Portland

Directions: From Highway 77 in South Portland, turn east on Broadway and after 1.4 miles turn left on Pickett Street. Turn left onto Pickett Street, which becomes Madison Street and leads to Bug Light Park, and a short walk to the to the light.

Coordinates: 43°39'19.9"N 70°14'05.5"W

Opened: 1875

Automated: 1934

Deactivated: Active

Lens: 250mm lens

Height: 26 feet

Focal Height: 30 feet

Signal: White flash every 4 seconds

Visitor Access: Grounds open, tower closed

Portland Head Lighthouse

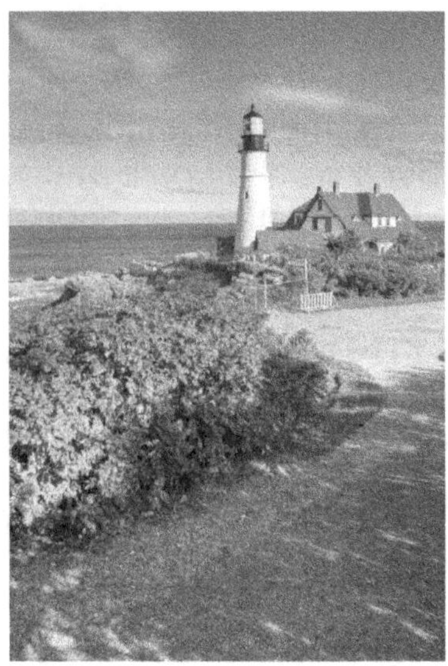

The Portland Head Lighthouse was opened in 1791 at the direction of George Washington. It is the first lighthouse built by the United States and the oldest one in Maine. It is also a very popular destination for visitors due to its very picturesque setting. In 1813 repairs were made to the tower whose upper portion was felt to be poor quality. In 1816 a passageway was built between the dwelling and the tower as the open ground was treacherous in winter.
A second-order Fresnel lens was installed in 1865. A new fog-bell tower was built to replace one destroyed in a 1869 storm.

The station was listed with the National Register of Historic Places on April 24, 1973.

Description: White tower

Location: Entrance into Portland Harbor

Directions: From Interstate 295 in Portland, take Highway 77 south to Broadway and go east on Broadway for 0.2 mi and turn right onto Cottage Road. After 1 mi, Cottage Road becomes Shore Road, which lead to Fort Williams SP and the lighthouse.

Coordinates: 43°37'23.2"N 70°12'28.3"W

Opened: 1791

Automated: 1989

Deactivated: Active

Lens: VRB-25

Height: 80 feet

Focal Height: 101 feet

Signal: White flash every 4 seconds

Foghorn Signal: 1 blast every 15 seconds

Visitor Access: Grounds open, tower closed.

Prospect Harbor Lighthouse

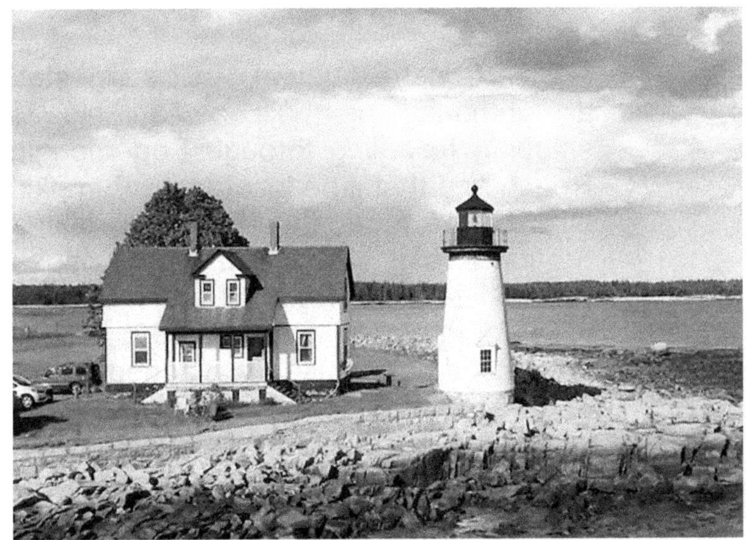

The Prospect Harbor Station opened in 1849 when a granite conical tower attached to a keeper's dwelling was built. It was built for shipping using Prospect Harbor. However the light was deactivated in 1859 when the Lighthouse Board felt it was not needed. It was reactivated in 1870 but by 1889 the station was reported in poor condition and in 1891 a 38 foot wooden tower and a new dwelling were built.

An oil house was built in 1905 and the light was upgraded to a fourth-order Fresnel lens the next year.

In 2022 a fire broke out in the dwelling but it was restored in a few months. The station was listed in the National Register of Historic Places on March 14, 1988

Description: White conical tower

Location: Prospect Harbor

Directions: From Gouldsboro, turn south on Highway 186 and in 5 mi you will reach Prospect Harbor. Turn east on Highway 195 and in 0.2 miles turn right on Lighthouse Road, which leads to the Naval installation where the station can be seen at the front gate.

Coordinates: 44°24'11.8"N 68°00'46.0"W

Opened: 1891

Automated: 1934

Deactivated: 1859-1870, reactivated 1870

Height: 38 feet

Focal Height: 42 feet

Lens: 250mm lens

Signal: Red flash every 6 seconds with white sectors, lit 24 hours

Visitor Access: Grounds and tower closed.

Pumpkin Island Lighthouse

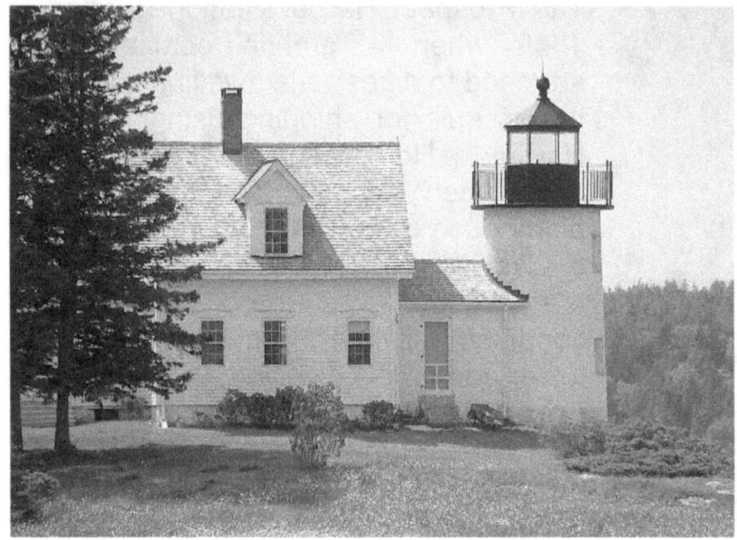

A U.S. Coast Survey in 1952 suggested a lighthouse be built as an aid to shipping travelling through Eggemoggin Reach and that it be located on Pumpkin Island. In 1854 the Pumpkin Island Station was established. It was equipped with a fifth-order Fresnel lens and later to a fourth-order one.. In 1906 an oil house and boathouse were added.
The station was deactivated in 1933 and in 1934 it was sold to a private owner and it remains so today.

The station was listed on the National Register of Historic Places on February 1, 1988.

Description: Conical tower

Location: Pumpkin Island

Directions: From Orland, go south on Highway 175 for 22.2 miles to Black Corner and turn right on Highway 15. Continue south for 3 mi to Little Deer Isle. Turn right on Eggemoggin Rd and after for 2.6 mi you will see the lighthouse.

Coordinates: 44°18'33.3"N 68°44'34.2"W

Opened: 1855

Deactivated: 1933

Height: 17 feet

Focal Height: 27 feet

Lens: Fourth-order Fresnel lens

Visitor Access: Grounds and tower closed

Ram Island Ledge Lighthouse

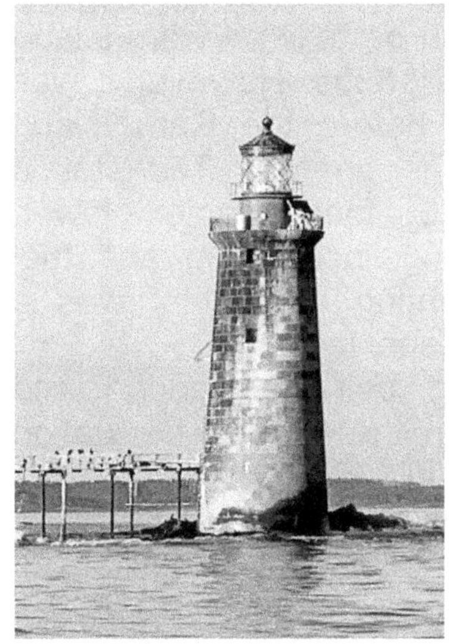

Ram Island Ledge Lighthouse was opened in 1905 to mark the north end of the main channel to Portland harbor. The initial lighting was a third-order Fresnel lens.
The station was electrified in 1958 and automated in 1959 and the lighting was upgraded to a modern 300mm optic.
The station was sold to a private individual in 2010.

The lighthouse was listed on the National Register of Historic Places on March 14, 1988

Description: White tower

Location: Ledges south of Ram Island

Directions: Accessible by boat, distant view from Portland Head Lighthouse

Coordinates: 43°37'53.4"N 70°11'14.4"W

Opened: 1905

Automated: 1959

Deactivated: Active

Lens: VLB-44

Height: 90 feet

Focal Height: 77 feet

Signal: Red flash every 6 seconds with 2 white sectors

Foghorn Signal: 1 blast every 3 seconds

Visitor Access: Grounds and tower closed

Ram Island Lighthouse

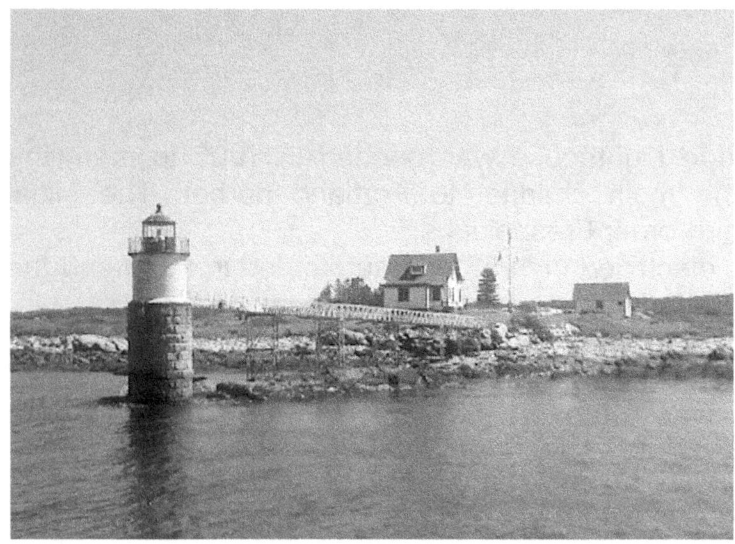

Interested parties had recommended that a lighthouse be built on Ram Island as early as the 1830s. However it was not until 1883 before the Ram Island Lighthouse was opened. The station included a 36 foot granite tower, keeper's dwelling, boathouse and fuel house. The lighting equipment was a fourth-order Fresnel lens.

In 1897 a fog bell was added and suspended from the tower. The station was automated in 1965

Listed on the National Register of Historic Places on January 21, 1988

Description: White tower

Location: Ram Island

Directions: Accessible by boat

Coordinates: 43°48'14.3"N 69°35'57.6"W

Opened: 1883

Automated: 1965

Deactivated: Active

Height: 40 feet

Focal Height: 36 feet

Lens: 250mm lens

Signal: Red flash every 6 seconds with two white sectors

Foghorn Signal: 1 blast every 30 seconds

Visitor Access: Grounds and tower closed

Rockland Harbor Breakwater Lighthouse

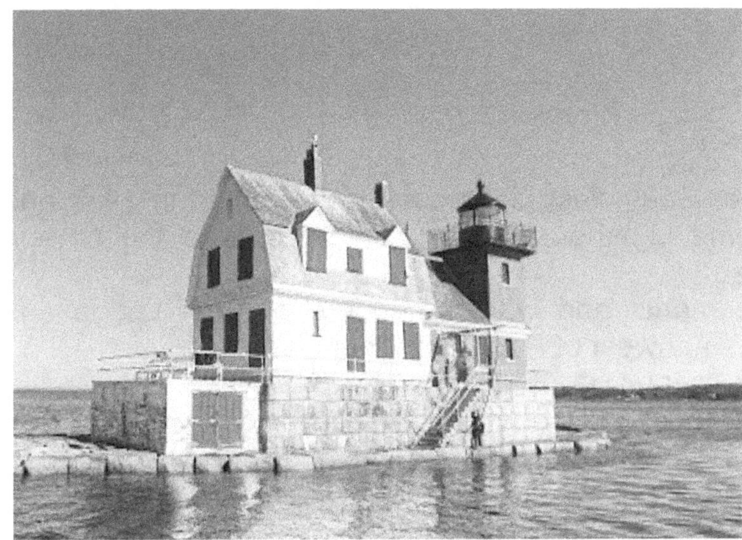

In 1889 a long breakwater was built at the mouth of Rockland harbor as an aid to the large number of ships using it. Initial plans had called for a lighthouse at the tip of the breakwater but cost overruns meant the lighthouse was not erected until 1902. The light was equipped with a fourth-order Fresnel lens as well as Daboll trumpet fog signal.

The station was automated in 1965 and the Fresnel lens was replaced with a VRB-25. From 2001-2011 the volunteers of the American Lighthouse Foundation restored the station.

Listed on the National Register of Historic Places on March 20, 1981

Description: Red brick tower

Location: Breakwater in Rockland Harbor

Directions: From Highway 1 north of Rockland, turn east on Waldo Ave and drive a half mile to Samoset Rd. Turn right on Samoset and go 0.6 miles to the foot of the breakwater.

Coordinates: 44°06'14.6"N 69°04'39.2"W

Opened: 1902

Automated: 1965

Deactivated: Active

Height: 25 feet

Focal Height: 39 feet

Lens: VRB-25

Signal: White flash every 5 seconds

Foghorn Signal: 1 blast every 15 seconds

Visitor Access: Grounds and tower closed

Rockland Harbor Southwest Lighthouse

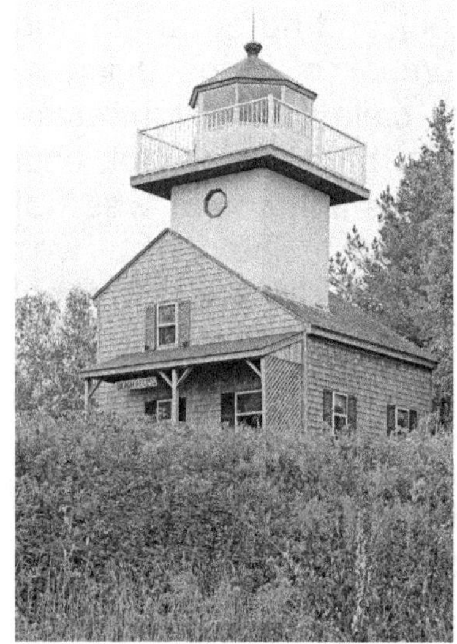

Rockland Harbor Southwest Lighthouse was erected in 1987 and is the only Maine Lighthouse built privately. This is the newest Maine lighthouse.
The lighthouse marks and warns mariners of Seal Ledge and shallow waters southwest of Rockland Inner Harbor.

The station was listed on the National Register of Historic Places on March 20, 1981

Description: Square gray tower

Location: Southwest shore of Rockland Harbor

Directions: From Rockland, go south on Highway 73 for 1.9 mi to North Shore Drive and turn left on North Shore Drive. Drive for 0.9 miles, and turn left on Shearmans Lane, a dirt road which leads to the light.

Coordinates: 44°04'57.7"N 69°05'46.6"W

Opened: 1987

Automated: 1987

Deactivated: Active

Lens: VRB-25

Height: 18 feet

Focal Height: 44 feet

Signal: Yellow flash every 2.5 seconds

Visitor Access: Grounds and tower closed

Saddleback Ledge Lighthouse

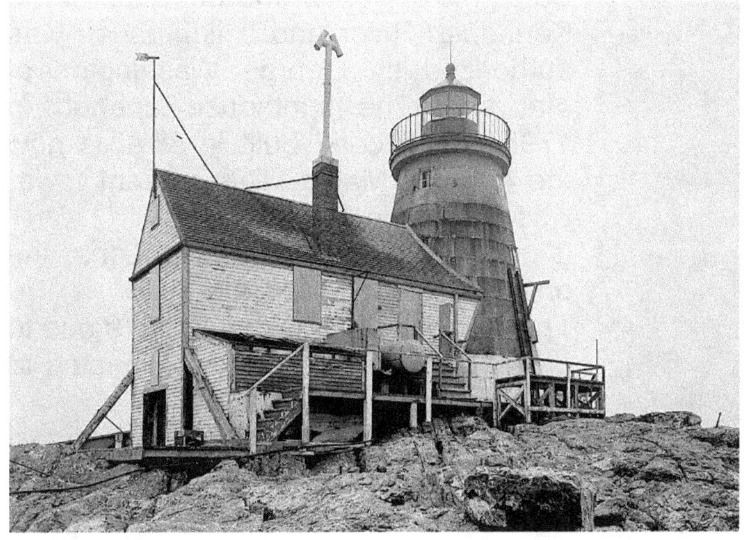

Saddleback Ledge is a rock of twenty feet situated at the entrance to Isle au Haut Bay. A lighthouse was suggested for the rock as an aid to ships using the harbor and in 1839 a conical tower made of granite blocks was opened. It has a focal plane of 52 feet above sea level.
The lighting equipment was upgraded to a fifth-order Fresnel lens in 1856 and to a fourth-order Fresnel in 1914. In 1867 a boathouse and addition to the dwelling were added. A fog bell tower and bell were added to the station in 1867, Saddleback Ledge Lighthouse was automated in 1954. Listed with the National Register of Historic Places on March 14, 1988.

Description: Gray conical tower

Location: Rock ledge between Vinalhaven Island and Isle au Haut

Directions: Accessible by boat

Coordinates: 44°00'51.6"N 68°43'35.2"W

Opened: 1839

Automated: 1954

Deactivated: Active

Height: 43 feet

Focal Height: 52 feet

Lens: VLB-44

Signal: White flash every 6 seconds

Foghorn Signal: 1 blast every 10 seconds

Visitor Access: Grounds and tower closed

Seguin Island Lighthouse

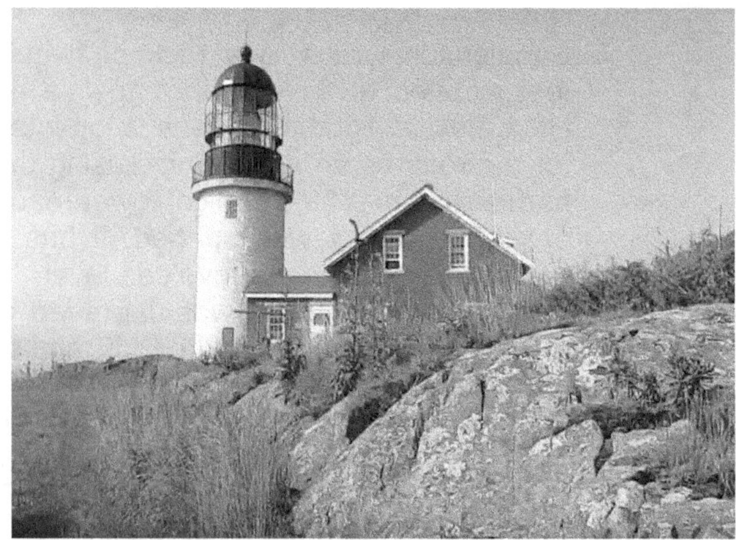

Seguin Island is off the entrance of the Kennebec River and a lighthouse was authorized by George Washington at that site. The lighthouse opened in 1795, the second built in what is now the state of Maine. The present tower was opened in 1857.

It uses a first-order Fresnel Lens, the only one used in the state.

The site was deactivated in 2019 due to power cable problems, but expected to be reactivated in future.

The station was listed in the National Register of Historic Places on March 08, 1977.

Description: White conical tower

Location: Seguin Island

Directions: Accessible by boat

Coordinates: 43°42'27.1"N 69°45'29.2"W

Opened: 1857

Automated: 1985

Deactivated: Deactivated in 2019 due to power cable problems, should be reactivated in future

Height: 53 feet

Focal Height: 186 feet

Lens: First-order Fresnel lens

Signal: Fixed white

Foghorn Signal: 2 blasts every 20 seconds

Visitor Access: Grounds open, tower open from Memorial Day through Labor Day

Spring Point Ledge Lighthouse

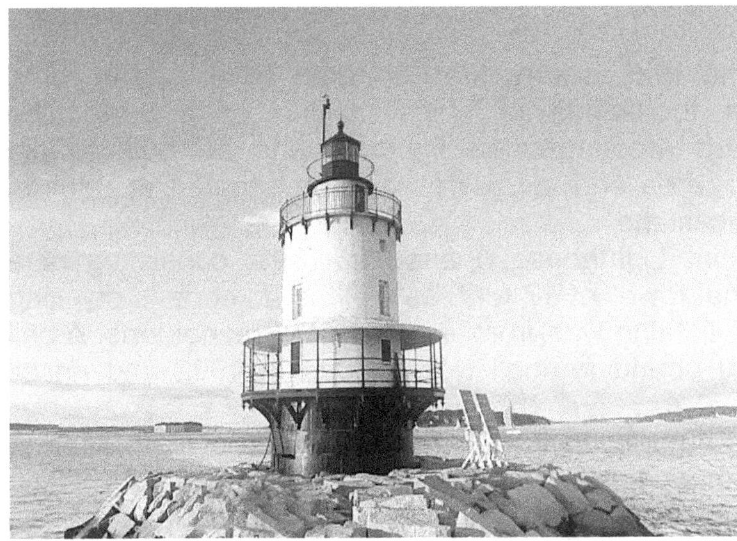

Spring Point Ledge in the entrance to Portland Harbor had represented a danger to shipping for many years. In 1897 a lighthouse opened at the site equipped with a fifth-order Fresnel lens. The structure had a cellar for coal, as well as a kitchen and rooms for the keepers.

The station was automated in 1960 and the lighting upgraded to a modern 300mm lens at that time.

Listed with National Register of Historic Places on January 21, 1988

Description: White tower

Location: Breakwater near the entrance to Portland's harbor

Directions: From Interstate 295, take Exit 6A and turn right on State Street (Route 77). Follow State Street through Portland to the stop sign in front of the marina. Turn right on Pickett St. then left on Fort Road to the end and the lighthouse.

Coordinates: 43°39'07.7"N 70°13'26.2"W

Opened: 1897

Automated: 1960

Deactivated: Active

Height: 54 feet

Focal Height: 54 feet

Lens: 300mm lens

Signal: White flash every 6 seconds with 2 red sectors

Foghorn Signal: 1 blast every 10 seconds

Visitor Access: Grounds open, tower open in summer

Squirrel Point Lighthouse

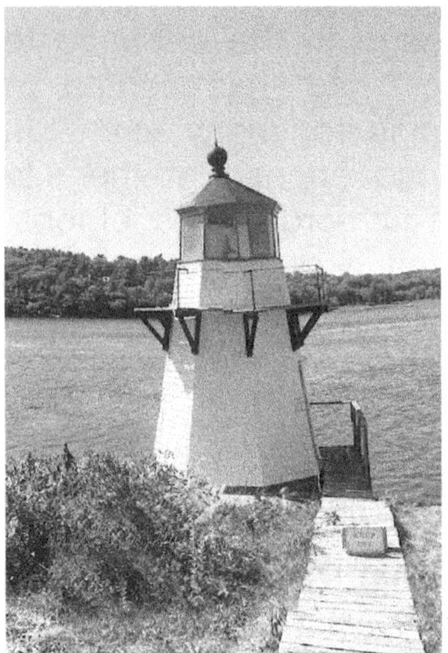

By the end of the 19th century, the Kennebec River had become very busy with thousands of ships visiting each year. The Lighthouse Board recommended light stations be built to aid navigation in the area and suggested one be situated at Squirrel Point on Arrowsic Island.

The Squirrel Point Lighthouse opened in 1898, consisting of a wooden octagonal tower of 17 feet, as well as a keeper's dwelling and a barn. The lighting was from a fifth-order Fresnel lens. A bell house and 1000 pound fog-bell were added in 1902 and an oil house in 1906.

The station was automated in 1981 and received a restoration in 2019. The station was listed with the National Register of Historic Places on January 21, 1988.

Description: White octagonal tower

Location: Southern end of Arrowsic Island

Directions: From Highway 1, take Highway 127 (Five Islands Road) south for 4 miles to Bald Head Road. Turn right on Bald Head Rd and drive 3 miles where you will find a path of a half mile to the lighthouse.

Coordinates: 43°48'59.7"N 69°48'08.8"W

Opened: 1898

Automated: 1981

Deactivated: Active

Lens: 250mm lens

Height: 17 feet

Focal Height: 25 feet

Signal: Red flash every 6 seconds with white sector

Foghorn Signal: 1 blast every 10 seconds

Visitor Access: Grounds open and tower closed

Tenants Harbor Lighthouse

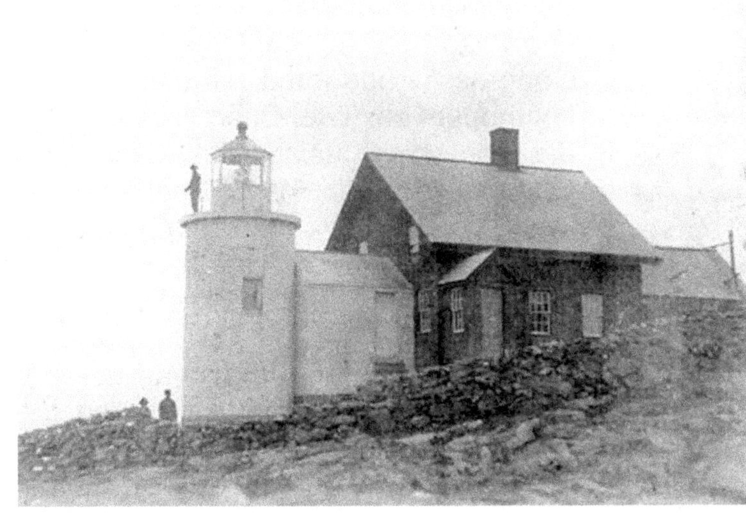

The Tenants Harbor Lighthouse opened in 1857 as a navigation aid for vessels using the harbor. It included a 27 foot brick tower and an attached keeper's dwelling.

Initially the lighting was a fourth-order Fresnel lens but this was changed to a fifth-order Fresnel lens in 1863. The signal was changed to a fixed red with a red flash once a minute.

A boathouse was added in 1880, a fuel house in 1895 and an oil house in 1906. The station was deactivated in 1933, and sold to the painter, Andrew Wyeth, in 1978. The station was listed on National Register of Historic Places on November 20, 1987.

Description: Cylindrical tower

Location: Southern Island

Directions: Accessible by boat

Coordinates: 43°57'40.0"N 69°11'05.4"W

Opened: 1857

Deactivated: 1933

Height: 27 feet

Focal Height: 66 feet

Lens: Fifth-order Fresnel lens

Signal: Fixed red with a red flash once a minute

Foghorn Signal: 1 blast, 30 seconds of silence, a double blast, 30 seconds of silence

Visitor Access: Grounds and tower closed

Two Bush Island Lighthouse

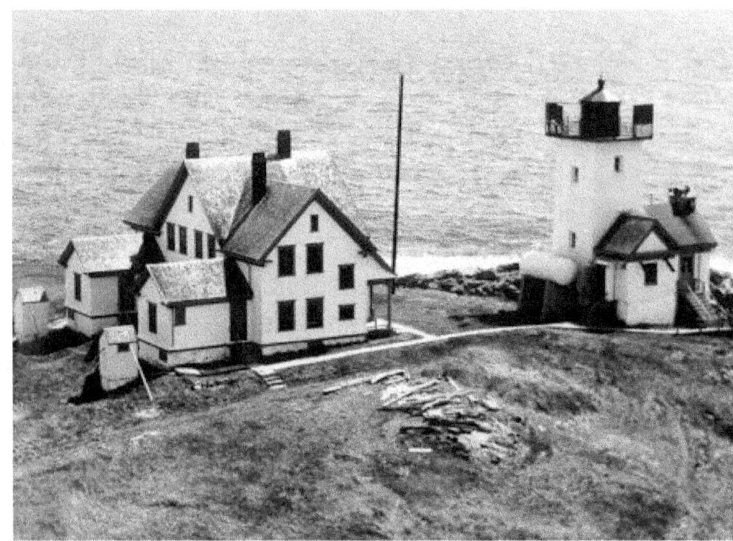

Two Bush island was named for two bushes on the island which were well know to ship's captains. In 1894, Congress budgeted funds for a lighthouse on Two Bush Island as an aid to ships using the Two Bush Channel to enter West Penobscot Bay. The Two Bush Island Station opened in 1897 and included a square brick tower of 42 feet, a keeper's dwelling and a boathouse.

A fifth-order Fresnel lens was used for lighting initially but this was upgraded to a fourth-order lens in 1902.

The station was automated in 1964.

Description: Square white tower

Location: Two Bush Island

Directions: Accessible by boat

Coordinates: 43°57'51.7"N 69°04'25.5"W

Opened: 1897

Automated: 1964

Deactivated: Active

Height: 42 feet

Focal Height: 65 feet

Lens: VRB-25

Signal: White flash every 5 seconds

Foghorn Signal: 1 blast every 15 seconds

Visitor Access: Grounds closed during seabird nesting season, tower closed

West Quoddy Head Lighthouse

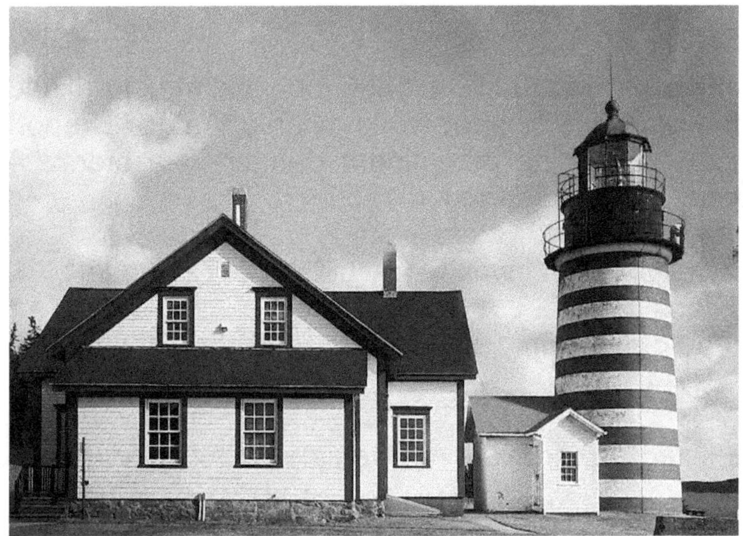

In 1808, Congress budgeted funds to erect a lighthouse at West Passamaquoddy Head to aid mariners to the harbor of Passamaquoddy. The West Quoddy Head Lighthouse is a conical tower of 49 feet high and equipped with a third-order Fresnel lens.

By 1831 the lighthouse had declined to the point that a new tower was built. However by 1857 the current tower was built as the second tower was in poor condition. The lighting was upgraded to a third-order Fresnel lens at that time and a new dwelling was erected.

In 1866 a fog trumpet was added to the station and was upgraded several times. The station was electrified in 1934 and automated in 1988. The station was listed on the National Register of Historic Places on July 4, 1980

Description: White tower with red stripe

Location: West Quoddy State Park

Directions: From Route 1 in Whiting, go east on hwy 189 for 10 mi turn south on Boot Cove Rd. After 2.8 mi, turns east on Quoddy Head Rd. into Quoddy Head SP, and the lighthouse.

Coordinates: 44°48'54.4"N 66°57'02.4"W

Opened: 1857

Automated: 1988

Deactivated: Active

Height: 49 feet

Focal Height: 83 feet

Lens: Third-order Fresnel lens

Signal: 2 white flashes every 15 seconds with red sector

Foghorn Signal: 2 blasts every 30 seconds

Visitor Access: Grounds open, tower closed

Whaleback Lighthouse

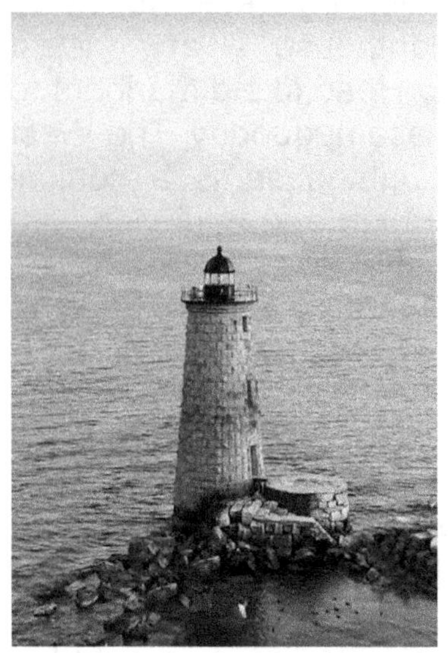

The original lighthouse was built in 1830 but the structure had problems from the start due to poor workmanship. An 1842 report described the tower as being in eminent danger in a storm. A fourth-order Fresnel lens was added in 1855.

A replacement tower of 20 feet was finally built in 1872 and in 1878 a bell tower was constructed.
The station was automated in 1963 and in 2009 the lighting was upgraded to a VLB-44.

The station was listed on the National Register of Historic Places on March 23, 1988.

Description: Conical tower

Location: Entrance to Portsmouth Harbor

Directions: Accessible by boat

Coordinates: 43°03'31.6"N 70°41'46.7"W

Opened: 1872

Automated: 1963

Deactivated: Active

Lens: VLB-44

Height: 70 feet

Focal Height: 59 feet

Signal: 2 white flashes every 10 seconds

Foghorn Signal: 2 blasts every 30 seconds

Visitor Access: Grounds and tower closed

Whitehead Lighthouse

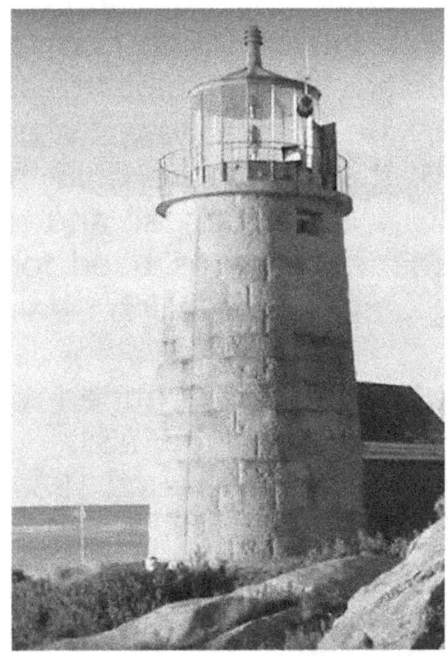

Mariners had requested a light on Whitehead Island since the 1790s as protection for ships sailing to Penobscot Bay. A station was opened there in 1807 consisting of an octagonal, wooden tower and a keeper's dwelling. This structure was replaced in 1931 with a 29 foot tapered tower and a new keeper's dwelling. In 1830 a fog building equipped with a new design of fog bell powered by the sea waves was added.
The current tower opened in 1852 consisting of a granite tower of 41 feet. The station was electrified in 1933 and automated in 1982

Listed in the National Register of Historic Places on March 14, 1988.

Description: Gray Granite tower

Location: Whitehead Island

Directions: Accessible by boat

Coordinates: 43°58'43.3"N 69°07'27.5"W

Opened: 1852

Automated: 1982

Deactivated: Active

Lens: VLB-44

Height: 41 feet

Focal Height: 75 feet

Signal: Green flash every 4 seconds

Foghorn Signal: 2 blasts every 30 seconds

Visitor Access: Grounds and tower closed

Whitlocks Mill Lighthouse

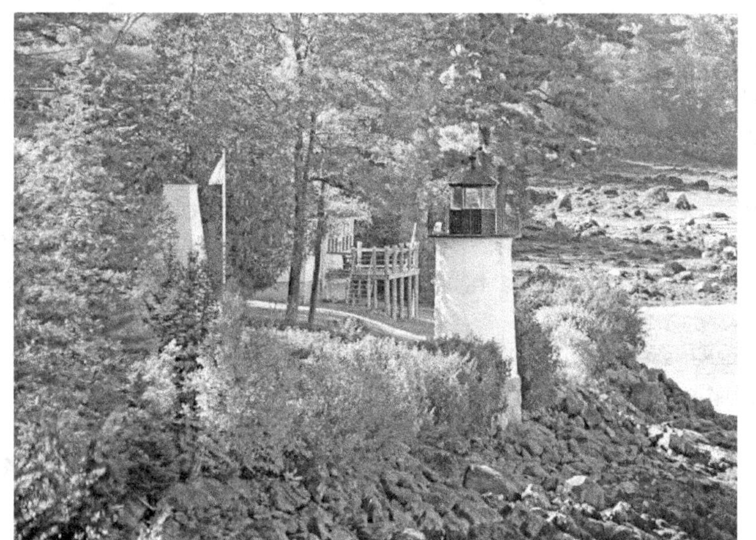

Whitlock Mill station was opened in 1892 when a red lantern hung from a tree was erected to aid shipping at Calais Harbor. The current tower was first lit in 1909, the last to be built in Maine. The tower is 25 feet tall and a fourth-order Fresnel lens was used for lighting. The keeper's dwelling was built in 1910.
An oil house and shed were added to the station, and a bell tower in 1931.
The station was electrified around 1931 and automated in 1969.

The station was added to the National Register of Historic Places as Whitlocks Mill Light Station on January 21, 1988.

Description: Gray cylindrical tower

Location: St. Croix River

Directions: View from picnic area alongside Route 1, roughly 2.5 miles south of Calais

Coordinates: 45°09'45.4"N 67°13'38.6"W

Opened: 1910

Automated: 1969

Deactivated: Active

Height: 25 feet

Focal Height: 32 feet

Lens: VLB-44

Signal: Green flash every 6 seconds

Visitor Access: Grounds and tower closed, privately owned

Winter Harbor Lighthouse

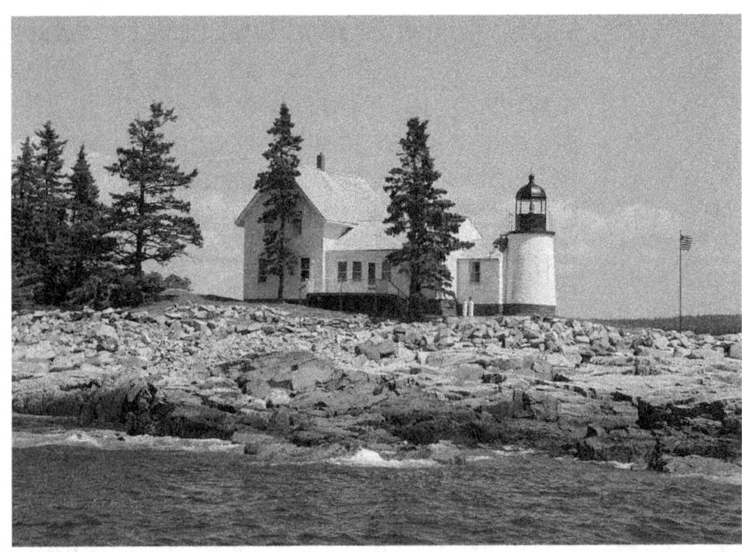

Congress budgeted funds to build a lighthouse to mark the entrance to Frenchman Bay and Winter Harbor Light was opened in 1857. It was located on Mark Island and the station consists of a 19 foot tower, a keeper's dwelling, a boathouse built in 1878 and an oilhouse built in 1905.
The station was deactivated in 1933 and sold into private hands the following year.

Listed on the National Register of Historic Places on February 1, 1988

Description: White conical tower

Location: Mark Island

Directions: From Highway 1 west of West Gouldsboro, turn south on Highway 186 and after 7 mi and turn right on Moore Road. After 1.4 miles you will enter the Acadia NP.
The lighthouse will be visible on an island offshore in 1 mi.

Coordinates: 44°21'41.2"N 68°05'15.5"W

Opened: 1857

Deactivated: 1933

Height: 19 feet

Lens: Fifth-order Fresnel lens

Visitor Access: Grounds and tower closed, privately owned

Wood Island Lighthouse

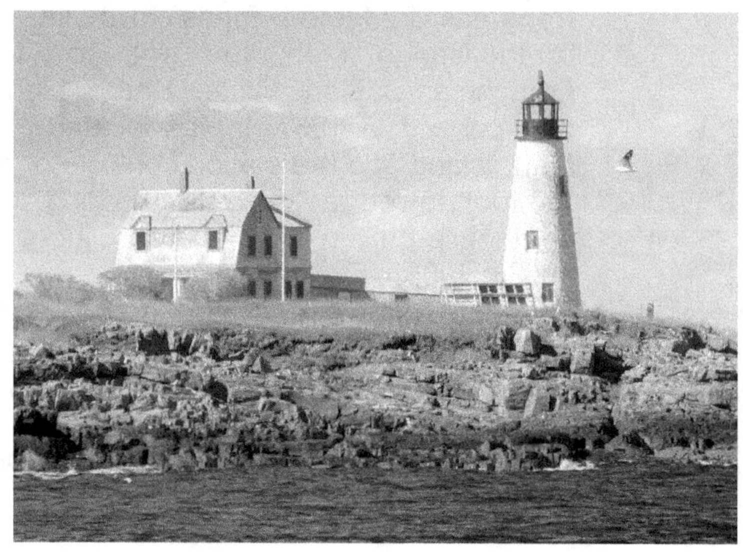

Wood Island Station was built on Wood island in 1808 as an aid to ships travelling to Biddleford Pool. It is the second oldest station opened in Maine. It consisted of an octagonal wooden tower and a keeper's dwelling.

In 1839 a new 47 foot stone lighthouse replaced the original which had deteriorated. In 1858 a new dwelling was erected as well as a fog signal tower. A fourth-order Fresnel lens upgraded the lighting.

In 1986 the station was automated.

The station was listed on the National Register of Historic Places on January 21, 1988.

Description: White conical tower connected to dwelling

Location: Wood Island

Directions: Accessible by boat

Coordinates: 43°27'24.6"N 70°19'44.4"W

Opened: 1839

Automated: 1986

Deactivated: Active

Height: 47 feet

Focal Height: 71 feet

Lens: VLB-44

Signal: Alternating white and green lights every 10 seconds

Foghorn Signal: 2 blasts every 30 seconds

Visitor Access: Grounds and tower open in season

Tours: Southern Region

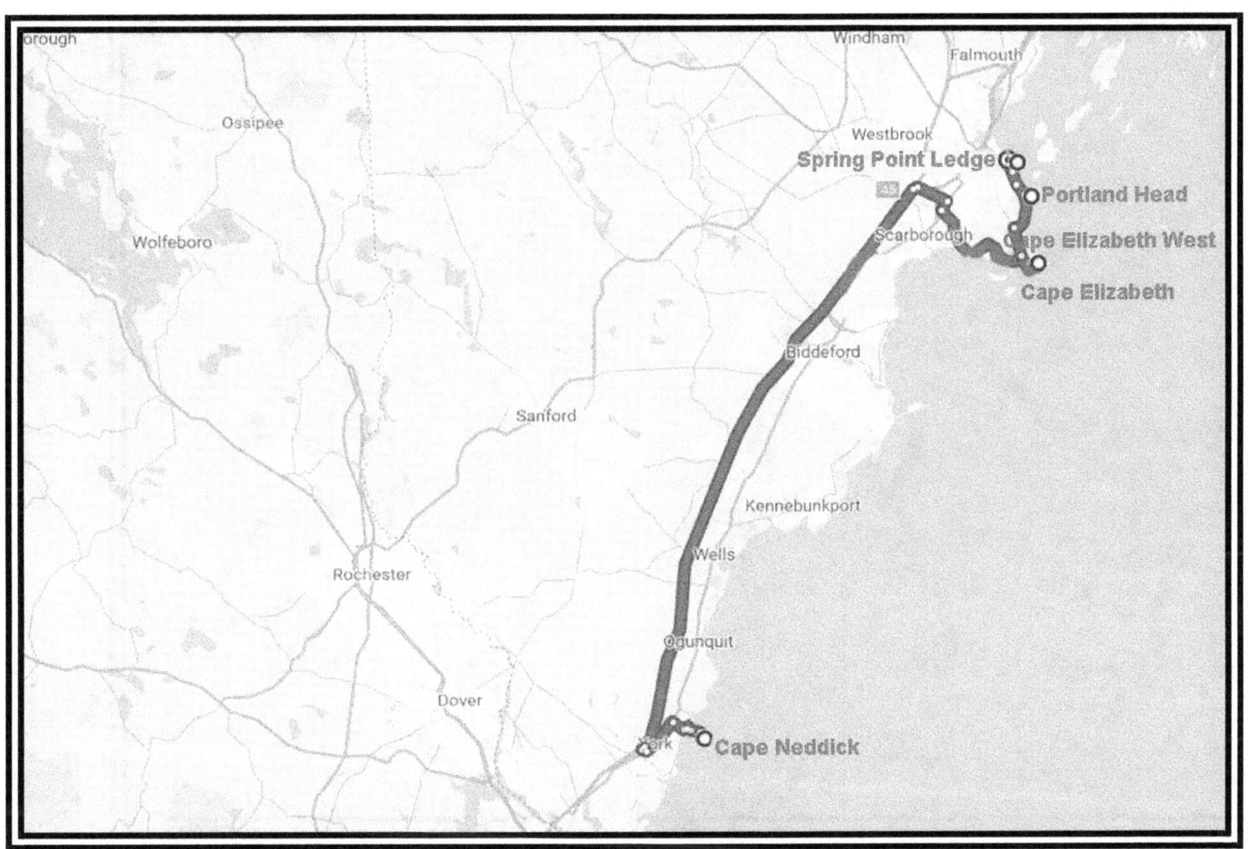

This tour is of 6 lighthouses and involves approximately 1.5 hours of driving

Cape Neddick	43°09'54.6"N 70°35'28.0"W
Cape Elizabeth West	43°33'51.2"N 70°12'09.3"W
Cape Elizabeth	43°33'57.9"N 70°12'00.3"W
Portland Head	43°37'23.2"N 70°12'28.3"W
Spring Point Ledge	43°39'07.7"N 70°13'26.2"W
Portland Breakwater	43°39'19.9"N 70°14'05.5"W

Tour: Central Region

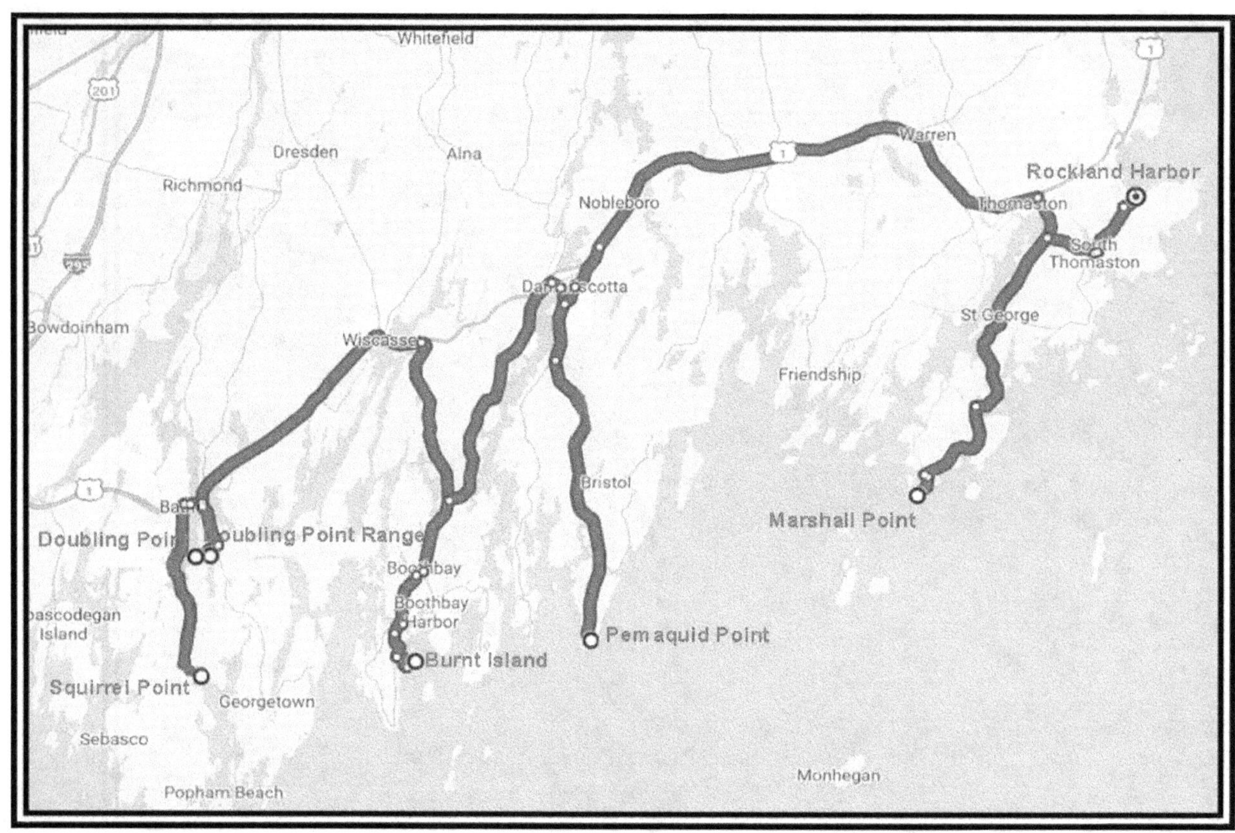

This tour is of 8 lighthouses and involves approximately 4 hours of driving

Squirrel Point	43°48'59.7"N 69°48'08.8"W
Doubling Point	43°52'57.1"N 69°48'24.2"W
Doubling Point Range (2)	43°52'58.3"N 69°47'44.4"W
Burnt Island	43°49'30.7"N 69°38'24.7"W
Pemaquid Point	43°50'13.1"N 69°30'21.8"W
Marshall Point	43°55'02.7"N 69°15'40.6"W
Rockland Harbor Southwest	44°04'57.7"N 69°05'46.6"W

Tour: Northern Region

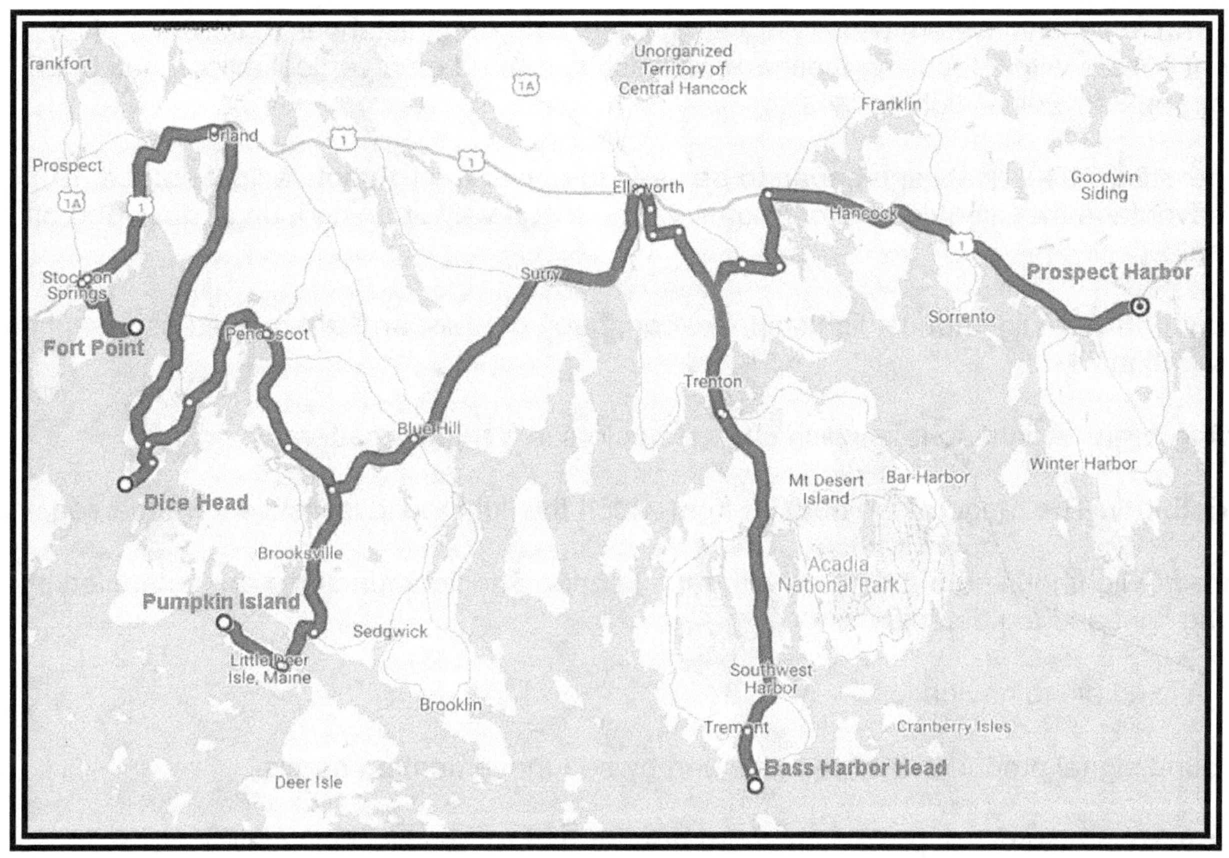

This tour is of 5 lighthouses and involves approximately 4 hours of driving

Fort Point Light	44°28'02.0"N 68°48'42.0"W
Dice Head Light	44°22'58.3"N 68°49'08.4"W
Pumpkin Island Light	44°18'33.3"N 68°44'34.2"W
Bass Harbor Head Light	44°13'18.5"N 68°20'14.3"W
Prospect Harbor Light	44°24'11.8"N 68°00'46.0"W

Glossary of Lighthouse Terms

Aerobeacon: A lighting system which creates a signal over long distances. It consists of a strong light source with a focusing mechanism which is rotated on a vertical axis. It has been used at airports as well as lighthouses.

Acetylene: After 1910, acetylene began to be used to power the lighthouse light source. It has the advantage that it could be stored on site with a sun valve turning it on at dusk and off at daybreak.

Aid to Navigation: A lighthouse, lightship, beacon, buoy or other apparatus used as an aid to ships navigation

Alternating Light: A light source which changes colors in a regular pattern.

Arc of Visibility: The range of the horizon from which the lighthouse is visible from the sea.

Automated: A lighthouse that operates without a keeper. The light functions are controlled by timers, and light and fog detectors.

Beacon: A fixed aid to navigation.

Bell: A sound signal produced by fixed aids and by sea movement on buoys.

Breakwater: A structure that protects a shore area or harbour by blocking waves.

Bull's-eye Lens: A convex lens used to refract light.

Caisson Tower: A hollow receptacle which can be filled with sand, stone or cement to act as a stable level base for a structure.

Catwalk: An elevated walkway which allows the keeper to move in the lantern room in towers built in the sea.

Characteristic: The distinct pattern of the flashing light or foghorn blast which allows seamen to distinguish which light station it is coming from.

Chariot: A wheeled assembly at the bottom of a Fresnel lens which is rotated around a circular track.

Clockwork Mechanism: Early lighthouses had a series of gears, pulleys and weights, which had to be wound on a recurring basis by the keepers.

Cottage Style Lighthouse: A lighthouse made up of a keeper's residence with a light on top.

Crib: A base structure filled with stone which acted as the foundation for the structure built on top.

Daymark: A unique colour pattern that identifies a specific lighthouse during the day.

Decommissioned: A lighthouse that has discontinued operating as a aid to navigation.

Diaphone: A sound signal produced by a slotted piston moved by compressed air.

Directional Light: A light which marks the direction to be followed.

Eclipse: The interval between light flashed or foghorn blasts.

Fixed Light: A light shining continuously without periods of eclipse or darkness.

Flashing Light: Alight pattern distinguished by periods of eclipse or darkness.

Focal Plane: The path of a beam of light emitted from a lighthouse. The height from the center of the beam to the sea is known as the height of the focal plane.

Fog Detector: A device used to automatically determine conditions which may reduce visibility and the need to start a sound signal.

Fog Signal: An audible device such as a bell or horn that warns seamen during period of fog when the light would be ineffective.

Fresnel Lens: An optic system composed of a convex lens and prisms which concentrate the light beam through a series of prisms. The design was produced by Augustin Fresnel in the 1800s.

Geographic Range: The longest distance the curvature of the earth allows an object of a certain height to be seen.

Isophase Light: A light in which the duration of light and darkness are equal.

Keeper: The person responsible for the maintenance and operation of the lighthouse.

Lamp and Reflector: A lamp and polished mirror used before the invention of more effective optic systems such as the Fresnel lens.

Lantern: A glass covered space at the top of the lighthouse tower, which housed the lighting equipment.

Lens: The glass optical system used to concentrate and direct the light.

Light Sector: The arc over which a light can be seen from the sea.

Lightship: A ship that served as a lighthouse.

Light Station: The lighthouse tower as well as any outbuildings such as the keeper's quarters, fog-signal building, fuel storage building and boathouse.

Nautical Mile: A unit of distance which is the average distance on the Earth's surface represented by one minute of latitude. It is equal to 1.1508 statute miles and mainly used at sea.

Nominal Range: The distance a light can be seen in good weather.

Occulting Light: A light in which the period of light is longer than the period of darkness and in which the intervals of darkness are all equal. Also known as an eclipsing light.

Order: A description of the power of the Fresnel lens ranging from one to seven from stronger to weaker.

Parabolic Reflector: A metal bowl shaped to a parabolic curve which reflects a lamp's light from it's center.

Parapet: A railed walkway which surrounds the lamp room.

Period: The total time for one cycle of the pattern of the light or sound signal.

Pharologist: A person with an interest in lighthouses.

Range Lights: Two lights which form a range provide direction to mariners for safe passage. They are described as the Front and Rear Lighthouses or the Inner and Outer. The front range light is lower than the rear, and when they align,the ship is in the proper position.

Revetment: A bank of stone laid to protect a structure against erosion from waves.

Revolving Light: A flash produced by the rotation of a Fresnel lens.

Riprap: Broken rocks or stone placed to help prevent erosion.

Sector: The portion of the sea lit by a sector light.

Skeleton Tower: Towers consisting of four or more braced feet with a beacon on top. They have little resistance to the wind and waves, and bear up well in a storm.

Solar-powered Optic: Many automated lights are run on solar powered batteries.

Spider Lamp: A brass container holding oil and solid wicks.

Tender: A ship which services lighthouses.

Ventilator: Opening' at the top of a lighthouse tower to provide heat exhaust and air flow within the tower.

VLB-44: The VRB-25 LED is a high intensity beacon which can be programmed for various lighting functions such as color, period and duration.

VRB-25: The VRB-25 LED is a high intensity rotating beacon with a range up to 25 nautical miles.

Wick Solid: A solid cord which draws fuel to the flame in spider lamps.

Photo Credits

Canadian Coast Guard, *Machias Seal Island,* **Centpacrr**, *Dice Head,* **Chriscoop**, *Egg Rock,* **Christina Lemieux**, *Little River,* **Dennis Jarvis**, *Curtis Island, Doubling Point Range, Lubec Channel, Rockland Harbour Southwest, Whitlocks Mill,* **Dk69**, *Boon Island,* **Dougtone**, *Doubling Point Range,* **DrStew82**, *Pumpkin Island,* **Hermann Thiersch,** *Tower of Alexandria***,** **Hidden Fox**, *Wood Island,* **Jamesl Woodward**, *Doubling Point, Perkins Island, Pond Island,* **Jeremy D'Entremont**, *Blue Hill Bay,* **Kevin A. Trostle**, *Baker Island* , **King of Hearts**, *Sandy Hook,* **Kyle MacLea**, *Grindle Point,* **Lee Coursey**, *Mount Desert Rock,* **Lvklock**, *Fort Point,* **Michele Dorsey Walfred**, *Winter Harbor,* **Mainiac,** *Monhegan Island,* **National Archives**, *Franklin Island,* **National Park Service**, *Bear Island, Public Domain, Halfway Rock, Moose Peak, Alexandria, The Tower of Hercules,* **ShagVT**, *Burnt Island,* **Ted Kerwin**, *Hendricks Head,* **U.S. Coast Guard**, *Heron Neck, Narraguagus, Tenants Harbor, Two Bush Island,* **U.S. Fish and Wildlife**, *Libby, Matinicus Rock,* **U.S. National Park**, *Saddleback Ledge*

All other images by the author

The Photographer's and Explorer's Series

Unless noted, there are Print and eBook editions available for the following.

Birding Guide to Orkney
Guide to Photographing Birds
Maine Lighthouses
Ontario Lighthouses
Ontario's Old Mills
Ontario Waterfalls
Alabama Covered Bridges (eBook)
California Covered Bridges (eBook)
Connecticut Covered Bridges (eBook)
Georgia Covered Bridges (eBook)
Indiana Covered Bridges
Maine Covered Bridges (eBook)
Massachusetts Covered Bridges (eBook)
Michigan Covered Bridges (eBook)
New Brunswick Covered Bridges
New England Covered Bridges
Covered Bridges of the Mid-Atlantic
Covered Bridges of the South
New Hampshire Covered Bridges
New York Covered Bridges
Ohio's Covered Bridges
Oregon Covered Bridges
The Covered Bridges of Kentucky (eBook)
The Covered Bridges of Kentucky and Tennessee
The Covered Bridges of Tennessee (eBook)
Vermont's Covered Bridges
The Covered Bridges of Virginia (eBook)
The Covered Bridges of Virginia and West Virginia
Washington Covered Bridges (eBook)
The Covered Bridges of West Virginia (eBook)

References

Coast Guard Light List
https://navcen.uscg.gov/sites/default/files/pdf/lightLists/LightList_V1_2023.pdf

Wikipedia list of Lighthouses in Maine
https://en.wikipedia.org/wiki/List_of_lighthouses_in_Maine

Maine Lights Today
https://www.mainelightstoday.com/light/

Lighthouse Friends
https://www.lighthousefriends.com/pull-state.asp?state=ME&Submit=Go

Lighthouse Digest
https://www.foghornpublishing.com/index.cfm

Index

www.ingramcontent.com/pod-product-compliance
Lightning Source LLC
LaVergne TN
LVHW080327110826
845155LV00026B/213

* 9 7 8 1 9 2 7 8 3 5 3 6 4 *